Doctor Robert Lefever

The Promis Re

C000252725

compulsive
helping

PROMIS

Written by Dr Robert Lefever

PROMIS Recovery Centre Limited
The Old Court House, Pinners Hill
Nonington, Nr. Canterbury
Kent CT15 4LL. UK
www.promis.co.uk

© Dr Robert Lefever 2005

ISBN 1 871013 22 4

Design and production by Rainbow, Ipswich IP5 3RY, England.
Printed in Basauri, Spain by Grafo SA.

**To
my wife, Meg who
helped me to face my reality
when she faced her own**

Acknowledgements

To my secretary, Sarah Oaten, for typing the manuscript

To my editor, Dr Harriet Harvey Wood for her helpful suggestions

To Keith Burns for proof-reading

To my wife, Meg, for running the family programme at PROMIS Recovery Centre and for knowing that tough love is still loving even though it may be tough when we first learn the difference between true helping and compulsive helping.

Contents

Nothing in all the world is more dangerous than sincere ignorance and conscientious stupidity.

Martin Luther King

Chapter One

Compulsive Helping: Who, Me?

How can helping be harmful?

Not all helping is harmful. In the right place, and at the right time, helping is a gift. Helping becomes harmful when it steps over the dividing line between caring (which is healthy and respectful) and care-taking (which is unhealthy and patronising and which does too much for other people, often diminishing their capacity to take responsible action).

What is the difference between helpful helping and compulsive helping?

We are truly helpful when we care for and respect the other people in our lives – but do not step over the boundary into taking on their responsibilities for them, which is what happens when we help compulsively.

In normal helping, we feel good when we focus appropriately on caring for other people but we still have time and energy for ourselves. In compulsive helping, we run other people's lives for them and we take the focus off running our own lives.

In compulsive helping we are relatively unaware of anything other than what we are doing for other people. Whether they are family members, friends or strangers, addicts or otherwise, that blind obsession with the perceived needs of other people, however well intentioned it may be, is compulsive helping.

How will we know when we are helping compulsively?

By being aware of our own selves, our own feelings, wishes and needs, we shall know when we take the focus off our own behaviour and put it on to other people's.

But we may not have addicts in our lives.

We can help other people compulsively regardless of whether they have addictive problems. As it usually turns out, those people who do not have addiction problems will probably become irritated if we turn our compulsive helping on to them, because it will diminish their own responsibilities. People who are leading a balanced life will not wish to have those responsibilities taken over – unless of course there are extenuating circumstances such as acute illness. It is unhealthy when people who are perfectly well physically, and fully competent in other ways, allow others to help them compulsively.

But we give help to people who need it.

The plain fact is that no one needs to be helped compulsively. Of course we can help others, in a caring, non-intrusive way, but compulsive helping does not do that. It gets in the way of a good, healthy relationship and it is therefore inevitably destructive.

But if we don't help, who will?

The short answer is that maybe other compulsive helpers will do so, or maybe the people we are trying to help will take responsibility for themselves, which would be the better option. Either way, as far as we are concerned, we need to keep out of the way and learn to look after ourselves. We need to be sure to keep to the normal, healthy, caring side of the compulsive helping boundary.

What is the difference between caring and care-taking?
Caring is friendly, loving, supportive and healthy. Care-taking, however, is over-caring for other people, taking on their responsibilities and not allowing them to learn from the consequences of their own actions or inactions.

Helping is loving, isn't it?
Helping is loving but compulsive helping is ultimately destructive of both ourselves and the person we are trying to help. That is not a loving action.

Isn't it good to put others first?
Sometimes it is. When people are too young, too old or too frail to be able to care for themselves, there are a number of things that would generally be considered to be helpful and caring. However, always putting our own needs last, never putting our own point of view in a discussion and always going with the flow of what everyone else appears to want, would inevitably be destructive of our own lives and a bad example to our families and to others.

How do we stop saying yes?
For compulsive helpers, this is one of the most difficult things to do. We like to say yes because we may believe that if we say yes, then the other people in our lives will benefit and they will appreciate us. We may find it difficult to say no because they might be cross with us or be disappointed in us. We would rather put up with the consequences of saying yes, and make sure that everyone else is happy, even if we ourselves are not. It then becomes progressively more difficult to start saying no, because those who know us will come to expect us to be there for them and to say yes to almost everything they want.

But what about what we want? What happens to us?
Failure to consider these questions is the equivalent of emotional suicide.

We therefore have to learn to start saying no, to be prepared to weather the inevitable storms that will arise in the short term and know that our relationships will gradually move to a healthier balance between the wants and needs of all.

How can we stand by and watch?
Watch what? The worst-case scenario is watching someone who is an addict destroy himself or herself because the helper in his or her life has stopped the compulsion to help, and is now standing back, leaving the addict to take the full consequences of his or her actions.

But we don't merely stand by and watch. We can go to meetings of Helpers Anonymous, meet friends, talk about any subject on earth *except* that of addiction, go for a walk, go to the cinema, an art gallery or concert hall or anywhere else that would brighten our own spirits. Then we take responsibility for ourselves and lead full and healthy lives in spite of any number of unsolved problems.

Just because we detach from trying to sort out other people's problems for them, this does not mean that we are uncaring. On the contrary, it is one of the most caring things we can do for other people when we leave them with the responsibilities of their own lives and then get on with managing our own lives. In this way, other people have the dignity and satisfaction of learning from their own experience and taking credit for their own achievements.

But they might die.
Yes, they might. But when we stand back and examine whether the help that we have been giving has actually been helpful, we may discover that it has not been helpful at all. We may then criticise ourselves for not giving enough help, or for not doing it in the right way; but our best efforts still fail. This is extremely hard for compulsive helpers to accept. Even more difficult is the recognition that our help may even be counter-productive: the more we do, the less the other people do for themselves and the worse things become. That way lies the probability, not merely the possibility, of death. Compulsive helping makes things worse, not better.

Why should we not help when we know what to do?
This is the ultimate arrogance of compulsive helpers. Who are we to know what is necessarily best for other people? What is so special about the way that we would run other people's lives, as opposed to the choices that they would make for themselves?

We're friends; why shouldn't we help?
As friends we can show love and concern and we can say how we feel; but compulsive helping destroys healthy relationships. It patronises and attempts to control. That is neither friendly nor helpful.

Chapter Two
Normal Helping

Dr William Glasser, on the first page of his book *Choice Theory* (Harper Perennial 1998), says, "When someone says 'I know what's good for you', we should run for our lives". He is absolutely right, the arrogance of compulsive helping can lead to considerable damage.

One might imagine that compulsive helping would damage only the individual that does it. He or she would become exhausted after doing so much "good" work. But there is another side to this, exactly as Dr William Glasser illustrates. Compulsive helpers have so much belief in the unique correctness of their own vision that they go on giving their "help" long after it is shown to be manifestly unhelpful. As the quotation from Martin Luther King at the front of this book illustrates, sincere ignorance and conscientious stupidity can be utterly destructive. We need to be very careful indeed before we consider that we know what is good for other people.

Is our vision necessarily the best for somebody else? Might not other people have visions of their own that might be very different from ours? Even supposing our vision is ideal, would other people necessarily be helped in the long term if we do everything for them rather than leave them the benefit of discovering and implementing things for themselves? Compulsive helping, behind a smoke screen of good intentions and well-meaning personal philosophy, can be the very devil. However, this does not mean that one should never be helpful to others. What we need to do is to distinguish normal helping from compulsive helping; the help that genuinely helps from the compulsive helping that actually destroys. Normal helping is respectful of the recipient. It does not patronise or dominate. It considers and supports. A few examples may clarify this:

- When a child finds homework difficult, it is genuinely helpful to explain (if one can!) the principles through which the child can work out the correct answers. The compulsive helper would provide the correct answer or would spend hours explaining so much that the child becomes even more confused – or falls asleep.

- When someone has the 'flu, a normal helper would get a couple of aspirin and a glass of hot lemon juice and would offer to buy a newspaper or change the sheets on the bed. A compulsive helper would move in, ignoring his or her own risks or needs.

- When her husband is drunk yet again, a normal helper would leave him in the mess that he creates and would say that enough was enough. A compulsive helper would wonder what she herself had done wrong and would telephone her husband's employer to say that he has stomach ulcers.

- When his son gets into financial difficulties, the normal helper would offer to look at the accounts. The compulsive helper would demand to see them, would give sincere advice and would then pay off the debt (yet again).

- When a teacher is confronted by a disruptive class, the normal helper singles out one or two of the pupils, listens to their concerns, makes an appropriate response and gets on with the teaching. The compulsive helper sets up a forum in which every child can have his or her say and then presents a summary to the head teacher or to the teaching trade union representative.

- When a counsellor is tired and jaded, the normal helper counsellor realises that he or she has done too much and should take time to go to the theatre. The compulsive helper counsellor blames his or her "burnout" on the employing institution and says that more time should be given to supervision.

- When an employer is faced with a complaint that one of his or her staff has behaved inappropriately towards another, the normal helper hears the complaint, makes a formal record of it and follows whatever the established procedure may be. The compulsive helper deletes a whole day of appointments in order to hear as many viewpoints as possible – and then takes charge of the enquiry.

- When the solicitor hears a hard luck story, the normal helper wonders what the client did that led to this particular result. The compulsive helper wonders what everyone else did – and arranges for legal aid.

- When a patient threatens to commit suicide, the normal helper doctor says "I cannot stop you if that's what you intend to do but, if there is a part of you that wants to live, I'll work with that". The compulsive helper doctor says "That's terrible. My wife and I were intending to go to the theatre but I shall cancel that so as to spend a couple of hours with you".

- When a constituent complains of poor housing, the normal helper politician wonders how other people in the same street do so well in identical circumstances. The compulsive helper politician says "The government ought to do something".

In each case the normal helper is genuinely caring but then thinks before acting. He or she considers whether a particular course of action would be genuinely helpful or whether it would in fact be counter-productive by undermining the individual's capacity to work things out and learn from experience.

There is a risk that compulsive helpers, in trying to get rid of this destructive behaviour, could become totally uncaring and even callous in disregarding the needs of others. What they need to do is to recognise compulsive helping for what it is: an arrogant behaviour that belittles others. Then they should learn how to become normal helpers. This is easier said than done, but it is a truly worthwhile aim. Normal helping is constructive, supportive, considerate, kind, effective, all of this and more. The appropriate alternative to compulsive helping is genuine kindness rather than determinedly uncaring disregard.

As with any other addictive or compulsive behaviour, the goal of recovery from compulsive helping is to learn how to behave as other normal people behave. The compulsive gambler learns to take normal risks that would be taken by anyone else. The compulsive exerciser learns how to keep fit normally rather than excessively. The workaholic learns how to be productive rather than obsessed. The compulsive shopper or spender learns how to stay within a budget of what can be afforded. The relationship addict learns how to be respectful of the other person. In each of these behavioural addictions, the goal is not total abstinence – which would be impossible – but abstinence from using the behaviour addictively.

The alcoholic knows that abstinence means having no alcohol whatever to drink. The drug addict learns that any mood-altering chemical has to be shunned. The sufferer from an eating disorder knows that sugar and white flour have a stimulant effect that presses the "more" button. However, even in these cases of apparently simple physical addiction, there is always a behavioural component. The alcoholic needs to beware of environments that trigger nostalgic memories of alcohol-using days, the drug addict needs to beware of continuing relationships with other people who are still using drugs, the sufferer from an eating disorder needs to beware of buffets – where the portions we take can grow by the minute– and of becoming obsessed by body weight or shape. So it is with compulsive helpers; they need to learn to recognise the "buzz" that they get from doing something that they believe is helpful, particularly when it is at significant expense to themselves and when there is little evidence to show that the action was in fact helpful to the other person.

The recognition of that "buzz" is all-important. This is the hook for the compulsive behaviour. The apparent drive towards selflessness, sacrificing self on the altar of other people's need, is only half the story. The other half is the superior belief in the compulsive helper's own understanding and values. Behind the superficial meekness of the compulsive helper lurks the potential to become an inconsiderate tyrant; and this is not a pretty sight when exposed to the clear light of critical examination. To turn back from that and become a normal helper is indeed a tall order, but it is certainly possible and well worthwhile.

Chapter Three

The Need to be Needed

At core in each compulsive helper is the need to be needed. This is an addictive, compulsive behaviour in its own right. The need is never satisfied. It is progressive and destructive, like any other addictive behaviour.

As with other addicts, compulsive helpers are born, not made. This need to be needed can often be traced back to earliest childhood. It is common in addictive families. Addicts and compulsive helpers seek each other out: the addict's need to be "fixed" (to have the inner emptiness "in here" filled in by something or somebody "out there") is matched by the compulsive helper's need to be needed (to have someone "out there" appreciate what can be given from "in here").

As a result of this mutual need, addicts and compulsive helpers often marry each other, to produce the next generation of addicts and compulsive helpers. Thus, the genetic pool may be relatively small but it is self-perpetuating. For those of us who are addicts or compulsive helpers (or both at the same time), we may believe that everybody in the whole world has primary addictive or compulsive helping tendencies. This is not true; most of the population have neither. It is only in our own little world that everyone – or almost everyone – has these tendencies.

The vast majority of the population do not use addictive substances and processes in order to change a sense of inner emptiness. Correspondingly, they do not compulsively help in order to experience the need to be needed. They may drink alcohol or smoke cigarettes or use occasional illicit drugs, or worry about their weight or have a flutter on a horse race or do a bit of "retail therapy"; but all these are part of normal human experience, just as normal helping is part of normal human experience. 80% - 90% of the normal population may use addictive substances such as alcohol or processes such as risk-taking on occasions; but they are not primarily addicted to them. The difference between "normal" and "addictive" use is inside the individual, not in the substance or process itself. Correspondingly, the vast majority of the population are perfectly capable of helping without becoming compulsive helpers. Again the difference is inside the individuals rather than in the process itself. The urge to help is universal. The urge to help in order to feel better about oneself is not. It is restricted to compulsive helpers.

The two cardinal features of compulsive helping are care-taking (when caring goes too far) and self-denial (when little regard is left for self).

Care-taking stems from the belief that other people really do need the insights and assistance of the compulsive helper. There is the story of the normal person and the compulsive helper in a blank room from which there are two exits. The normal person opens one door and is hit on the head by a man holding a mallet. So the normal person retreats and subsequently goes to the other door, opens it and goes happily on his or her way to freedom. The compulsive helper goes to the first door and receives the same bash as the normal person had received. A few moments later he or she goes back to the same door and receives the same response. A few moments after that, the compulsive helper goes over to the exact same door for a third time and finds that the man is no longer there – so goes looking for him! Care-taking results in the compulsive helper being drawn like a magnet towards people who are destroying themselves and others. The need for help is manifest. The urge to help is overwhelming, irrespective of whether the end result is actually helpful.

Self-denial seems at first sight to be a worthy process. Certainly we abhor the boastful conceit of people who are utterly self-centred. However, the compulsive helper goes too far into the pit of altruism, denying self to such an extent that there may be little left of coherent personality and true independent values. It is often said that when a compulsive helper is drowning, someone else's life passes before his or her eyes.

Selflessness may appear to be a virtue but in the hands of a compulsive helper it becomes a useless sacrifice and a very poor example to others.

For the primary addict, blame and self-pity exactly correspond to the compulsive helper's care-taking and self-denial. The primary addict and the compulsive helper are each as sick as the other. Then each gets locked into the other's compulsive behaviour, so that each gets worse rather than better.

Of course it is possible for a compulsive helper to have normal, healthy relationships, but these do not satisfy the need to be needed. Therefore the compulsive helper tends to seek out addicts – those members of the community who tend to be most needful of all – just as the addicts tend to seek out compulsive helpers, the members of the community who are most likely to sacrifice themselves on the altar of helping others.

There is the common belief that these behaviours can be learned rather than genetically inherited. The Scandinavian evidence from adoption studies shows that alcoholism goes primarily with the genetic inheritance rather than with the environment of upbringing. The Vietnam war veterans study showed that most GIs were able to give up the drugs that they had used during that terrible conflict and could go back to "sensible" drinking and even the occasional, relatively harmless use of other addictive substances and processes. 10% could not do that, but remained addicted. Some people would see this latter group as being weak-willed, but there is no evidence of that in other aspects of their lives. Quite the contrary: they are often strong-willed to a fault. It seems more probable that the continuously addicted group had a genetic predisposition leading them to a dependency upon mood-altering substances and processes.

Perhaps some people are born with genetic defects in their neurotransmission systems. In the mood centres of the brain, the messages may not be sent accurately from one nerve cell to another. The chemicals that transmit these messages may not be secreted properly at one nerve ending or they may not arrive properly at another or they may leak out at the side of that junction. One way or another, the process may be defective so that the individual experiences a sense of inner emptiness *for no explicable reason.* This depression, or involutional melancholia, should be distinguished from sadness, which is the normal human response to upsetting events. The person suffering from neurotransmission disease, as I would term it, has no explanation whatever for feeling so depressed. He or she just does feel depressed. Then comes the magical discovery of a mood-altering substance or process or special relationship that lifts that mood. The effect may be only temporary but the experience is never forgotten. Repeated use results in repeated lift of the mood. Why on earth would that person ever elect to go back to the terrible inner emptiness previously experienced? Thus the addictive process takes root.

I should emphasise immediately that the appropriate treatment for the involutional melancholia of neurotransmission disease is *not* an anti-depressant medication. These drugs are inevitably addictive because of their mood-altering properties. They are slow to act and slow to produce withdrawal symptoms when their use is discontinued but the dependency can be very severe and they take away the natural spontaneity and colour of life – which is a terrible price to pay for a "treatment".

Considering neurotransmission disease, we should not express great surprise that the human brain, that most complex of all of our organs, should have some potential for genetic defects. After all, every other organ in the body has genetic defects associated with it. In the brain itself, we are aware of a number of genetic impairments that lead to defects of mental function. Surely it is inevitable that there will also be genetically inherited defects in the mood centres.

Our research at PROMIS, where we have treated over 3,500 in-patients suffering from various forms of addictive or compulsive behaviour over the last 19 years, shows that people who have addictive tendencies of one kind or another tend to have them in clusters as follows:

i.   Hedonistic: alcohol, recreational drugs, mood-altering prescription drugs, nicotine, caffeine, gambling and risk-taking, sex and love addiction.

ii.   Nurturant of self: food bingeing or starving, vomiting or purging, exercise, work, shopping or spending.

iii. Relationship addiction (using other people as if they were drugs) or compulsive helping (using self as a drug for other people).

Some people have just one of these groups of addictive outlets, others have two and some have all three.

In relationship addiction and in compulsive helping, there is a sub-division into dominant and submissive sub-groups. Each illustrates a particular form of emotional blackmail in the personal relationship. In the dominant group, the individual in effect says "Do what I tell you or I shall hurt you". Whereas in the submissive group the threat is "Do what I tell you or I shall hurt myself". Some people have clearly delineated tendencies, being always either dominant or submissive, whereas others may be dominant in some relationships (say, with a spouse or one parent) while being submissive in others (say, with a child or with the other parent).

It seems very improbable that there could be a gene relating to the addictive use of one particular substance – such as alcohol. From the evidence of our studies at PROMIS, however, it seems to me quite likely that there would be a "hedonistic" gene, leading people to say "To hell with it, let's do it", a "nurturant of self" gene, saying "I need something to soothe me" and an "addictive relationship/compulsive helping" gene saying "I need to bury myself in a relationship". Of course we can all do silly or self-destructive things by choice rather than from genetic drives, but it does appear from epidemiological studies (genetic studies are not yet available) that some people have particular drives towards addictive or compulsive behaviour.

Differentiating normal behaviour from addictive or compulsive behaviour is vital. The Shorter PROMIS Questionnaire attempts to do exactly that, looking at *why* people do things, rather than primarily at what specific substance they might use or when or in what quantity. The questions have to be framed carefully in order to distinguish accurately between normal and compulsive behaviour. There are as many risks in under-diagnosis as there are in over-diagnosis.

The questionnaires are based upon twelve specific addictive characteristics as follows:

1. Preoccupation with use or non-use.

2. Preference for, or contentment with, use alone.

3. Use as a "medicine", to help to relax or sedate or to stimulate.

4. Use primarily for mood-altering effect.

5. Protection of "supply", preferring to spend time, energy or money in this way.

6. Repeatedly using more than planned. The first use tends to trigger the next.

7. Having a higher capacity than other people for using the substance or process without obvious initial damaging effects, although in time this "tolerance" is lost.

8. Continuing to use despite progressively damaging consequences.

9. "Drug"-seeking behaviour, looking for opportunities to use, and progressively rejecting activities that preclude use.

10. "Drug"-dependent behaviour, "needing" the addictive substances or behaviour in order to function effectively.

11. The tendency to "cross-addict" into other addictive substances or processes when attempting to control our use.

12. Continuing to use despite the repeated serious concern of other people.

The original questionnaires asked 30 questions on each of 16 addictive outlets, including 2 on compulsive helping (dominant and submissive) and 2 on addictive relationships (dominant and submissive). Through further analysis, it was found that the top 10 answers giving the highest scores in each addictive tendency gave just as accurate a delineation of an addictive tendency as did the full 30 questions. The Shorter PROMIS Questionnaire that we now use is therefore only 160 questions long. It can be seen in full on the PROMIS website, **www.promis.co.uk**, which will also score the answers, giving comments on their significance to an addictive tendency.

The questionnaires for compulsive helping and relationship addiction are as follows:

In each case a total of up to 5 points should be allotted to each answer on the principle that zero means that this activity is of no significance, 5 indicates that it is highly significant and 1, 2, 3 or 4 indicates that it is something in between those two extremes. As a general principle, a total of 20 points on any one of the following 4 questionnaires indicates a level of addictive significance.

Compulsive Helping Dominant

1. I have been afraid that I would be thought of as (and perhaps become) a callous person if I do not show my capacity for self-denial and care-taking on a daily basis.

2. The things I have done for others have often resulted in there being not much left of my personal life.

3. I have preferred to look after other people on my own rather than as part of a team.

4. I have found life rather empty when someone for whom I was caring gets better, and I have felt resentful at times when I am no longer needed.

5. I have tended to use my self-denial and care-taking of others as both a comfort and strength for myself.

6. I have found that I tend to adopt a self-denying and care-taking role in many of my relationships.

7. I have regularly given unsolicited advice to other people on how to solve their problems.

8. I have found it difficult to leave any loose ends in a conversation in which I am trying to be helpful.

9. I have often stayed up half the night having "helpful" conversations.

10. I have felt that I become a real person only when I am tidying up the physical, emotional and social messes made by someone else.

Compulsive Helping Submissive

1. I have tended to pride myself on never being a burden to others.

2. Other people have tended to express concern that I am not doing enough for my own pleasure.

3. I have tried to avoid all risks of upsetting other people.

4. I have tended to give (an act of service to others) and not count the costs, even though the costs mount progressively.

5. I have tended to remain loyal and faithful regardless of what I may endure in a close relationship.

6. I have liked to make myself useful to other people even when they do not appreciate what I do.

7. I have tended to take on more work for someone close to me even if I have not finished the previous batch.

8. I have felt like a real person only when performing acts of service for someone else.

9. I have often helped someone close to me more than I intended.

10. I have felt most in control of my feelings when performing services of one kind or another for someone else.

Addictive Relationships Dominant
Four positive answers indicates the need for further assessment.

1. I have tended to look for, or take on, positions of power or influence so that I rise to a position of emotional or practical power over others as rapidly as possible.

2. I have found it difficult not to take up a position of power or influence when it is available, even when I did not really need it and could see no particular use for it.

3. I have preferred to have power and influence in all my relationships rather than allow myself to be vulnerable.

4. I have been afraid that my life would fall apart and that others would take advantage of me if I were to give up the power and influence that I have held or now hold.

5. I have regularly undermined other people's positions of power or influence even though they may have significantly less than my own.

6. I have found that having all the power and influence that I needed for my own personal and professional life has been irrelevant in deciding when to stop seeking more.

7. I have tended to use a position of power or influence as a comfort and strength, regardless of whether there have been particular problems needing my attention in other aspects of my life.

8. I have looked for all opportunities for power and influence as and when they arise.

9. In a new relationship I have felt uncomfortable until I hold the most powerful position.

10. I have tended to neglect other aspects of my life when I have felt that my position of power or influence has been under threat.

Addictive Relationships Submissive.
Four positive answers indicates the need for further assessment.

1. I have tended to be upset when someone close to me has taken care of someone else.

2. I have felt that I become a real person only when I am being totally looked after by someone else.

3. I have found that other people have tended to express progressively more concern about my dependent relationships.

4. I have tended to find someone else to be close to me when my primary partner has been away even for a short time.

5. I have tended to find a new close relationship within days or weeks of the failure of a previous one.

6. I have tended to venture into company only if I have someone to look after me.

7. I have felt an overwhelming sense of excitement when I have found a new person to look after my needs, or a new way in which an existing partner could look after them better.

8. I have tended to think that a close friendship is when someone else really looks after me.

9. I have tended to get irritable and impatient when people look after themselves rather than me.

10. I have felt most in control of my feelings when other people are performing services of one kind or another for me.

The crucial issue in assessing the significance of the answers to these questionnaires is to recognise that the normal, non-addictive population, tends to score very low – perhaps 3 or 4 points in total on each questionnaire and often a total of only 20 or 30 points out of a possible total of 800 on the entire 160 questions in the full questionnaire. Addicts commonly score 30 or 40 points or even a maximum of 50 points on individual questionnaires and may score 200 or 300 points or even more in total. Compulsive helpers often score 30 or 40 points on one of the compulsive helping questionnaires and may score equally heavily on the other. They may also score significantly on the relationship questionnaires and on some general addictive outlets. Thus there appears, from relatively sharp cut-off points on the total points on the answers to each questionnaire, to be a relatively clear dividing line between the normal population and the addicted population but not between compulsive helpers and primary addicts. It seems reasonable therefore to treat compulsive helping as just another compulsive or addictive tendency, the same as any other, even though "the need to be fixed" is the mirror image of "the need to be needed".

Chapter Four

The Magnetic Attraction of the Addict

Addicts and compulsive helpers are drawn to each other, like iron filings to a magnet. Frequently the divorced wife of one alcoholic will promptly marry another active alcoholic. Obviously one can see the advantages to the alcoholic in finding someone else to tidy up all the mess and listen to all the blather of self-pity and blame. The advantage to the compulsive helper is in setting out on a further crusade in the belief that he or she, perhaps uniquely, has something to offer and can save the wretch from doom. The same process can take place in any other addict/compulsive helper relationship. I recall the following:

- The father who repeatedly put money into his domestic safe even while knowing that his son was stealing it. The father's rationalisation – which perpetuated the son's addiction – was that it enabled the boy to buy drugs rather than steal them.

- The senior politician's wife who stayed in the shadow of the great man, breeding from him but ignoring her own intellectual and social interests while traipsing round the constituency day after day in support of his workaholism and general grandiosity.

- The sister who continued to pay for the alcoholic sister's treatment although blaming the treatment centre for failure to prevent each successive relapse. In this case the treatment centre staff may have been compulsively helping the patient, repeatedly re-admitting her and, at the same time, may have been taking advantage of the other sister's compulsive helping.

- The international singer's repeated justification of his daughter's drug addiction by claiming that it was due to manic depression.

- The businessman, whose sense of guilt for spending so much time amassing his wealth, spent huge amounts in compensating landlords and hoteliers for the incredible damage caused when his addicted son chose to trash their accommodation. The father kept the story out of the newspapers again and again – and the son went on doing it.

- The husband who repeatedly collected his alcoholic wife from treatment every time she complained that the therapeutic programme was too difficult – and then brought her back the next day when she was drunk yet again.

- The mother who brought heroin into a treatment centre for her son because she believed that he might be being detoxified too quickly.

- The Alcoholics Anonymous sponsor who had 16 sponsees, leaving herself little time for focused attention on her family or even at times for her work.

- The treatment centre director who said that nicotine addiction is not a necessary concern in primary treatment, despite knowing that it doubles the relapse rate in patients suffering from alcoholism or drug addiction.

- The mother who spent hours cutting up her anorexic daughter's food into small pieces and sitting with her, pleading with her to eat, day after day after day, in defiance of the observation that the girl was getting worse rather than better.

- The doctor who stuck to a diagnosis of depression, and continued to prescribe anti-depressants, despite the patient's obvious alcoholism which, in the doctor's view, would be a disgrace or evidence of weak will.

- The cardiologist who prescribed medications to lower her patients' cholesterol but did not confront them on their cigarette smoking.

- The counsellor who agreed with the patient that it would be difficult for her, an alcoholic school mistress, to be in the same therapeutic group as a pupil from another private school, despite the fact that she had been drunk repeatedly in front of pupils in her own school.

- The doctor who used her own hard-earned money to pay for the treatment of one of her patients rather than spend it on herself and her own family.

- The grandmother who repeatedly gave money to her granddaughter, denying that she could possibly be a drug addict.

- The retired banker who repeatedly paid his son's gambling debts, thus guaranteeing their recurrence.

- The husband who explained his wife's significant obesity by saying that "there must be something wrong with her glands" and denying that it could be due to overeating.

- The father who repeatedly blamed the schools for the academic failure of his addicted children.

- The man who set up a charity and gave so much time to it that he got divorced.

- The headmistress of a 1,000-pupil school who said "We have no drug addiction here".

In each of these examples there is obvious damage as a result of the primary addict's behaviour but the compulsive helper colludes with that behaviour so that it is not directly confronted.

Direct confrontation is the very thing that compulsive helpers find most difficult to do. They want to avoid it at all costs. This is perhaps understandable when their experience of attempting it has resulted in major hostile reaction. However, the question that then has to be asked is why the compulsive helper tolerated that major hostile reaction. The answers I have heard include "She doesn't really mean it", "He has these difficulties", "I am determined to show him a better way of doing things", "She's my wife", "He's only young", and so on and so on. Frequently there is a justification, a rationalisation, an excuse, exactly parallel to the rationalisations, justifications and excuses that active addicts of one kind or another give for their own destructive behaviour. In fact, very often the addicts themselves find that they no longer need to provide rationalisations, explanations and excuses: the compulsive helper will do that for them.

The magnetic attraction between the addict and the compulsive helper destroys the capacity for impartial observation and rational judgement. Obviously one expects this impaired judgement when the primary addict is under the influence of alcohol or drugs or other compulsive behaviour but it is no less true for the compulsive helper in the full throes of his or her absorbing behaviour. This same process can be seen when compulsive helping becomes institutionalised:

- Why does the government believe that banning cigarette advertising would reduce consumption rather than merely influence brand loyalty? After all, there is no advertising for cannabis or cocaine, yet these substances are very widely used.

- Why do schools expel their addicted pupils rather than provide treatment opportunities for them? Is it because they are in thrall to the parents or local authorities who believe that strict discipline could eradicate an emotional problem or is there a disorder of perception? Who is it who has the disorder of perception?

- Why do some hospital colleagues protect an alcoholic consultant by denying him access to hospital beds and thereby protect his patients but do nothing to help the man himself?

- Why do some politicians claim that the National Health Service is under-funded – and refuse to see that one could fund a Health Service on any budget whatever, provided one grasps the nettle of telling the electorate what one will not fund from within that budget?

In each case, the institutionalised compulsive helping has massively damaging consequences. The magnetic attraction of the compulsive helper to the addict is just as powerful institutionally as it is individually. Attitudes and ideas become enshrined in holy writ rather than remaining available to be challenged. Is the welfare state really such a good idea? Is the fact that it doesn't work in practice merely a product of under-funding and mismanagement – or is it based upon fundamentally flawed ideas that spring from collectivised compulsive helping? Is a fascist society, in which the weakest members go to the wall, if not to the gas chambers, really the only alternative?

The institutionalised blackmail of compulsive helping ideas need to be challenged just as forcefully as the individual compulsive helping ideas in a family or place of work. Wherever it occurs, compulsive helping needs to be confronted so that primary addiction can also be confronted rather than, in effect, assisted.

The power of the magnetic attraction is that the primary addicts and compulsive helpers are both genuinely in the grip of their illness. They may have occasional determined control over their behaviour on a day-to-day basis as it affects other people but they have no control over the underlying addictive urges. The compulsive helper understands primary addictive urges instinctively but then, through his or her own actions or inactions, makes the situation worse. The need to be needed is indeed a powerful magnetic force, drawing primary addicts to it in fatal attraction.

Chapter Five

Environmental and Cultural Influences

Whilst compulsive helping may be a genetically inherited defect of neurotransmission in the mood centres of the brain, there are none the less widespread cultural influences that tend to lead towards compulsive helping being admired and feted rather than acknowledged as such and feared.

- Childhood fairy stories perpetuate myths that the poor are always deserving and that employers or landlords are always cruel and greedy.

- "Green" environmental ideas are enshrined in our educational system from primary schools onwards. Bjorn Lomborg's book, The Skeptical Environmentalist (Cambridge, 2001), soundly based in scientific observation when it challenges these hallowed tenets, is criticised with a ferocity that is worthy of nature's own bared tooth and claw.

- When do the animal rights enthusiasts, who may equate the killing of animals with the murder of human beings, see that their own behaviour is just as blinkered and self-serving as the behaviour that they oppose?

- When do those who clamour for their rights – or for those of other selected groups within the general population – recognise that they also have responsibilities? When will they also recognise that the state has no resources of its own, only the confiscated resources of the productive private sector?

- When will "motherhood" be freed from superhuman expectations? To be associated with sainthood is poor compensation.

- When will "politically correct" ideas be seen often to be the perpetrators rather than confronters of prejudice?

Our society is riddled through and through with collectivist ideas that stem from compulsive helping origins. We believe that we should help other people, usually at someone else's expense. We know what is good for other people and often we insist that someone else should do it.

The concept of self-sacrifice, in the service of others, is so deeply imbedded in our culture that it is almost sacrilegious to challenge it. Yet why should *self-sacrifice* be admirable? Why should putting the needs of others *before* those of oneself be considered to be virtuous? Just how far should this principle be extended? To death? Who then will produce?

Ironically it is the compulsive helpers who often both demand and produce. On the one hand they proclaim the needs of other people who are "less fortunate" (never lazy or incompetent, self-willed or belligerent) and then demand that other compulsive helpers should do something to *make* things better. Politicised compulsive helping is a very scary monster whose inevitable ultimate end is totalitarianism.

It is extraordinary how much our society denigrates producers. We worship pop stars and other entertainers, professional sports men and women and television "personalities", but we denigrate our businessmen and women, taking it for granted that they are self-serving and greedy. Yet where would we be without the washing machines and vacuum cleaners, the new building materials and insulation systems, the antibiotics and hormone replacements, the central heating, pure water supply and efficient drainage, the telephone, fax and personal computer, the car and the television? "Environmentalists" – perhaps the most arrogant and demanding of all social groups – have their own idiosyncratic answers to these questions but few of us would wish to join them in their quest to re-establish the Middle Ages.

Yet still we perpetuate the myths that enshrine compulsive helping as a virtue, rather than see it as a potential vice. The care-taking and self-denial of compulsive helping are *not* virtues. More often than not, as I have illustrated, they do *not* improve the lot of other people. Frequently they lead to a learned dependency:

- The drug addict spends the Social Security cheque on more drugs, rather than on housing, food and clothing.

- The young unemployed who see no reason to work while the state will provide for them. They soon learn to develop the "medical" conditions that allow them to graduate from unemployment benefit to invalidity benefit. They learn how to work the system.

- The striking trade unionists who demand their "rights" – to blackmail the rest of the population into paying them more and more in return for less and less.

- The doctors who resent being assessed, because they believe that academic examination results from 20 years ago should guarantee them an indefinite licence to practise.

- The lawyers who believe that morality is indefinable, if not irrelevant, provided that they themselves get paid.

- The street beggars who discover that they make more money in this way than they would if they were to take more conventional employment.

- The academic, sitting in their ivory tower and protected from the harsh realities of the outside world, who demands that state subsidies should be increased because of the unique worthiness of his or her particular contribution to society.

- The theatre director who demands state subsidies for plays that vilify the very people who provide the tax revenue that pays the state subsidy.

The dependency culture is widespread within our community. It does not apply solely to single parents struggling to make ends meet while refusing to accept that it was often – but not always – their own behaviour that got them into that predicament. The welfare state is the embodiment of institutionalised compulsive helping. When we observe that it doesn't work in practice, we demand that it should have an increase in its budget, and in its powers, rather than a reduction. When we observe that those in greatest need are the ones least likely to receive state resources to help them, we may criticise the administrators, but we rarely offer to give up our own benefits. Yet why should the state ever help those who are perfectly capable of helping themselves? Why should challenge to the ideas of the welfare state itself – rather than to its organisation and implementation – be considered taboo? Only because compulsive helpers say so.

This does not mean that everyone who believes in, or who is involved in running, the welfare state is necessarily a compulsive helper. However, it does mean that we should all of us challenge any idea that can be seen to be deficient in practice. In particular, we need to shrug off the guilt that compulsive helpers would like us to wear, even if they choose to wear it themselves.

Chapter Six

Politics and Religion

It is perfectly possible to be a member of a "helping" profession without being a compulsive helper. Similarly, it is perfectly possible to work in a bar without being an alcoholic. In each case, the addictive behaviour does not come as a result of working in a particular profession or environment. Nor is it a requirement for the job. However, in each case, the people who have that particular addictive tendency – compulsive helping or alcoholism – would be quite likely to seek employment where they would feel at home with their addictive tendency and where other people would be more likely to praise it than criticise it or be concerned by it.

In two professions in particular – politics and religion – there is almost an expectation by other people that these individuals *should* be compulsive helpers. We expect our clergy to be self-sacrificial, slaughtering themselves on the altar of self-denial and exhausting themselves spiritually and physically in the service of others. We expect our politicians – in return for the privilege of receiving our vote – to solve instantly any problem we ever have. We expect them to find limitless resources and divert them to the particular cause that we hold dear. In each case we expect clergy and politicians to be magic-makers rather than acknowledge that there are realistic limitations to what they can achieve.

To some extent clergy and politicians have only themselves to blame when they make out that they can achieve more than is humanly possible. The same may be true of doctors, nurses, health visitors, social workers, probation officers, teachers, lawyers and others who would broadly come under the classification of "professional helpers". In each case we may shy away from telling our patients, clients or students the limits of our capacity. Even we ourselves may want to avoid facing up to the limits of what we can achieve. We would always prefer to blame others – usually our professional representatives or the government itself – for inadequate funding or inefficient management.

The phrase "the government ought to do something" is very close to the lips of anyone living in a welfare state. We get used to believing that it is the government's responsibility to tidy up all the messes in society. We get into the habit of blaming the government rather than taking positive action ourselves to do something about the mess. We delegate politics to the politicians; religious or spiritual ideas to the clergy; medical responsibility to the doctors and nurses; the process of learning to teachers; the concept of the law – or of what we can get away with – to lawyers; and we delegate anything and everything we can to the government.

Into this moral vacuum steps a compulsive helper, with a need to be needed, sometimes also showing the characteristics of a relationship addict, with blinkered self-centredness and a craving for power and influence. Armed with self-righteousness, he or she sets about tackling all society's problems, taking responsibility for other people rather than simply being responsible to them. The last thing that a compulsive helper would ever contemplate is that people might be responsible for their own condition, particularly when it can be shown that others with equal lack of privilege or resources have achieved much more than the people on whose behalf the compulsive helper takes up the cudgels. Nowhere is this more obvious than with the clergy or politicians. The clergy – with some notable marvellous exceptions – surround themselves with the inadequate and ineffectual, declaring them to be under-privileged or downtrodden. Politicians – again with notable exceptions – may do the same. In this respect the clergy and the politicians often work together, heaping moral opprobrium on the rest of the population for being "uncaring" or even "fascist" when we do not share their priorities.

Yet who is it who benefits from the emotional blackmail of the do-gooders of church and state? It has to be said that sometimes the chosen recipients do indeed benefit – but certainly not all the time. However, the clergy and the politicians benefit every single time from the status they award themselves as "feeling" or "caring" or "understanding" or "insightful" beings – and the rest of the population very often buy into this.

We would be wise to avoid giving any profession the accolade "caring". Doctors should do their professional work, becoming better technicians – perhaps especially in the field of human psychology – rather than using a mask of "caring" behind which to hide incompetence or arrogance. The clergy should focus upon individual spirituality and unhinge themselves from the corporate welfare state. Politicians should focus upon discussing what can be achieved within an inevitably limited budget, rather than for ever promising Utopia in response to the demands of the electorate. The electorate itself – and its equivalents as patients, pupils, congregations, recipients of welfare or what have you – should see *first of all*, for the sake of their own dignity and long-term emotional and physical well-being, what they can do for themselves.

Unquestionably there are people who have very little capacity to look after themselves. These are the very people who should have first call upon state resources. In practice they tend to be cared for primarily through charities such as the Salvation Army, Help the Aged, MIND, the Red Cross and others. Our society is extremely generous in what it gives to charities, despite the fact that we have a welfare state. Secretly we know that the welfare state does *not* care primarily for those most in need. Each one of us on the ladder looks to those above us in the taxation and welfare system to provide for us in our hour of need and we believe that our own taxes, such as they may be, do more than enough for those below us on the ladder. Thus the state itself creates an arid, uncaring society in which individual commitment and compassion takes second place. We may at times give to charity in place of doing something practical ourselves.

Again, the compulsive helper steps into the vacuum – and runs the charities, knowing what is best for other people. The pressure group and the single-issue fanatics illustrate compulsive helping at its worst. Again, this is not to say that all people who run charities, or who have particular social enthusiasms, are necessarily compulsive helpers. It is simply more likely that compulsive helpers, rather than other people, will seek those positions. They need to be needed. They want to demonstrate their human virtue and greater social understanding.

Religion and politics should perhaps be the highest callings. Perhaps they would be if we could find a way of keeping compulsive helpers out of them. Perhaps we could then focus upon what actually works in practice, rather than on what *should* work simply because it appears superficially to be virtuous.

Chapter Seven

Selfishness

Ayn Rand, in her book *The Virtue of Selfishness* (Penguin USA 1992), points out that it is bizarre that the word "selfish" should have come to be derogatory. Why would something related to one's own self-interest be considered unworthy? Why should it necessarily be at anyone else's expense? We need to examine who it is that benefits from twisting the word "selfish" to mean the opposite of what it should reasonably mean.

People who think and act for themselves, taking responsibility for themselves and not expecting others to provide for them, are a threat to the corporatist ideas of church and state. People who rely upon the enterprise, achievements and material wealth of others, in order to support their own chosen causes, are often resentful of the very people upon whom they depend. The state hides behind the "moral" sanction of the church in equating wealth with wickedness. Even the great philanthropists are seen as people who *owe* something to "society" (whatever that may be). In practice "society" is whatever the overlords of church and state deem it to be.

People (including compulsive helpers) who give away their own time and money and other resources are entitled to do so in whatever way they want. If they do it from the kindness of their hearts, then so much the better. If they do it in the hope of purchasing local adulation, or even a national political honour, then why ever not? These end results are harmless conceits and the honours system has largely been devalued through political chicanery in any case. The concern should not be over baubles but over banquets; the rewards that the leaders of church and state take to themselves, while demanding the redistribution of wealth created by others. Further, while the state depends upon confiscating wealth through taxation, the church supports the state in this legalised theft on the basis of morality! Further, if people keep their own money and other resources, and see no reason to share them, they are termed "selfish".

In practice it requires a great deal of skill and enterprise to accumulate wealth or even to keep it if one inherits it or is given it or wins it in some way. Stories of people going from riches to rags are as common as stories of those proceeding in the opposite direction. If we are to criticise those who look after their wealth, are we to praise those who throw it away?

Why should the poor necessarily be "deserving"? Do they necessarily benefit if rich people sell all they have and give to the poor merely in order to enter a "kingdom of heaven" defined by the church? Is it not more likely that the recipients of handouts will take them as their "rights" – and then demand even more? Are they encouraged by the leaders of church and state to give credit to those whose enterprise created the wealth that the state, encouraged by the church, confiscates and distributes? Or do those same leaders of church and state demand that they themselves should be praised and thanked for enforcing this "redistribution"?

Once one comes to examine the morality of socialised welfare systems, there are some very unattractive creatures creeping out from underneath the stones.

True compassion can only ever be individual. It is a human attribute. The moment that church and state become involved, it becomes subjugated to corporatist, religious or political ideas that are highly critical of individualism. After all, if individuals were to do things out of the kindness of their own hearts and because they want to do them voluntarily, there would be no need for the prelates of church or the presidents of state: they would be out of a job. For this reason, church and state have to keep expanding their activities and increasingly enshrine them in law in order to maintain their pre-eminent position as the givers of all good things. This is the practical cause of Ayn Rand's observation that the difference between a welfare state and a totalitarian state is merely a matter of time. On this same basis, it is interesting to note that in some political circles "charity" has become a dirty word. It smacks of Lady Bountiful, patronising the downtrodden poor. Yet charity is based upon voluntary gift, whereas the provision of services through the state is based upon enforced confiscation, with the ultimate threat of imprisonment. What morality is that?

In practice, vast numbers of people give voluntarily to charities, fully knowing that the state very often fails to provide for those most in need. Furthermore, the industrialists who create the wealth of our society are frequently vilified for doing so but nevertheless often establish charitable institutions, or give massive financial contributions to particular causes, over and above all the taxes that they have paid throughout their lives. Yet still they are often seen as being "selfish" simply because they are industrialists. Global capitalism, multi-nationalism – call it what you will – is seen in some political circles as being corrupt and self-serving. Indeed, it is exactly that when tariffs and industrial strength interfere with free markets. However, the alternative of state-run services leads inevitably to equivalent corruptions in power politics, with kick-backs and pay-offs of one kind or another. In all this maelstrom of deceit and corruption, the one shining light is individual talent, enterprise and compassion. "Selfishness" – accepting responsibility for self and doing what one believes is in one's self-interest – is the only thing that is dependable.

It is often argued – particularly by the leaders of church and state – that individual compassion cannot be relied upon. The evidence is to the contrary; vast private contributions are made each year even within a welfare state. People give to others when they do *not* need to do so and even while they are paying taxes. The fears of the leaders of church and state are that they themselves would be redundant in the absence of a welfare state. They turn the word "selfish" to mean the opposite of its true meaning. The truth is that our self-interest is best served when we create a kind and compassionate society – and give to it voluntarily. Our self-interest is certainly not served by ignoring the needs of those less fortunate than ourselves. The virtue of selfishness is that we discover what is truly in our own best interests by choosing to be kind, thoughtful and generous.

In the welfare state, we have come to believe that people have to be coerced, with threats of punishment, before they will do anything to help others. The reverse is true. Schools and hospitals and many other social institutions were often created through charitable donation. The welfare state subsequently nationalised many of them –with no compensation to the original donors – and, of all things, now takes credit for this theft! To the challenge that individual compassion could not be relied upon, the answer is that the state very often completely fails to provide for those most in need. While attempting to provide universal services, the state often fails to discriminate appropriately between those who can perfectly well look after themselves and those who genuinely need assistance. To the further challenge that private individuals could not possibly provide the level of resources currently provided through the welfare state, the appropriate response is that the welfare state is too big and very much *needs* to be cut back so that it focuses on what needs to be done.

Primarily what needs to be cut back is the power of church and state. Their emotional blackmail and financial coercion are a hindrance to the fostering of individual compassion. When people see that the state is not delivering the goods, they tend to say that it *should* do so rather than to ask what they themselves could do. True selfishness – seeing the benefits of individual contributions to society and reducing dependence upon the state – should be the way forward towards a kinder, mutually supporting and efficient society.

Compulsive helpers tend to buy into the emotional blackmail of the church and state and believe that they *should* do all sorts of things, if not in order to enter the kingdom of heaven then at least to be "good" people. Surely the way to be "good" people is to *do* something good rather than talk about it on a focus group, quango or charity, all of which specialise in allocating other people's time and money. Thus, normal helpers tend to get on and do something, whereas compulsive helpers often feel that they have to run the whole world to their own design in order to *make* it compassionate (as they would see it).

The two central features of compulsive helping – care-taking and self-denial – come into their full glory when the whole apparatus and finance of the state is available. Progressively more and more of the lives of individuals is usurped by the state when compulsive helpers feel that something *must* be done. Compulsive helpers exhaust themselves on committees, proving to the world that they are not "selfish" (in the negative way that term has come to be understood). If compulsive helpers thought less about other people and more about themselves, the world might indeed be a better place and the word "selfish" might return to its rightful place as a description of human virtue.

Chapter Eight

Compulsive Helping as an Addiction

Compulsive helping would be no great problem if it were simply a bad habit in which people indulged themselves every so often. The same would be true of drunkenness. Indeed, normal people do at times become insufferably bossy or get drunk. However, that does not make them into compulsive helpers or "temporary" alcoholics.

An addictive tendency is not simply a normal tendency taken to extremes. As emphasised in chapter three, addictive behaviour has specific characteristics that define it and that separate the addicted population from the normal population. Alcoholism and other addictive tendencies, including compulsive helping, are quite specific addictions and are therefore progressive and destructive. They are not temporary: they are permanent, probably genetically inherited. They are not something that can be shrugged off with new insights or determinedly put down with willpower. To be sure, alcoholics and compulsive helpers can force themselves into abstinence for a short time, but they do so at a terrible price to their emotional balance, becoming angry and resentful. This can become very confusing to other people, particularly if they believe that the problems go with the substances or processes rather than with an underlying individual predisposition. When the alcoholic or compulsive helper relapses to the former addictive behaviour, the acute tension dissolves, precisely because the "treatment" for the underlying mood disorder is now being received again.

This parallel, drawn between alcoholism and compulsive helping, is true for any addictive or compulsive behaviour. Indeed, if this behavioural pattern is not visible, and the answers to the PROMIS questionnaires are negative, then the behaviour is not addictive or compulsive. Some people just do get drunk, as part of their culture. Some people just are bossy and interfering, as part of their normal behaviour. Neither of these behaviours defines the individual as being an alcoholic or a compulsive helper. As previously emphasised, there is as much danger in over-diagnosis as there is in under-diagnosis.

Just as alcoholism becomes progressively worse as one gets older, or as a result of increased use, the same process can be observed in compulsive helpers; this addictive tendency is also progressive and destructive. In early life a compulsive helper may be thought of as being a thoroughly nice child, always willing and co-operative. As time goes on, the compulsive nature becomes apparent, with the young adult needing to get involved in various enterprises in order to improve self-esteem. At the same time, relationships will be formed, commonly with people who have the corresponding primary addictive inner emptiness and "the need to be fixed". These relationships, between the compulsive helper and the addict, become progressively more enmeshed as each partner attempts to solve all life's problems by focusing on the emotional dynamic of the relationship. The "need to be fixed" intertwines with the "need to be needed" and strangles any opportunity for normal spontaneity, creativity and enthusiasm. The sick relationship is the central focus of sick lives.

As time goes on, one relationship may disintegrate, only to be replaced by another that is equally sick. The quest for the perfect relationship seems to have been achieved after all – only for disappointment to set in yet again. Disillusion and despair become the order of the day, with the addict progressing further into blame and self-pity and the compulsive helper descending further into care-taking and self-denial.

In employment the addict does progressively less and less, often losing one job after another as a result of unreliable behaviour. Meanwhile the compulsive helper may do more and more, taking on extra burdens in order to try to compensate for the behaviour of the addict but also in order to feel more worthwhile, knowing that he or she is doing everything possible to *make* things better. In fact, what may be happening is that everything that is being done contributes towards things getting worse. Addicts get better when they take responsibility for themselves. Compulsive helpers get better when they stop doing anything and everything for everybody else and begin to do things that interest and please themselves, rather than solely in the determined service of others.

Eventually the addict is destroyed, either through the consequences of the use of addictive substances and processes or by their own hands, when they realise that they can no longer live with these addictive substances and processes but also cannot contemplate the emotional emptiness of life without them. By the same token, compulsive helpers progressively drain their lives of all colour. They become subservient to the demands of the addict or of other people in general. Their self-sacrifice is total; there is nothing left to be seen of any individuality. They may hide behind a profusion of good work and selfless commitment but, behind this facade, there is nothing there. The lights are on but there is nobody at home. There may be the superficial busy-busy-busy-ness of endless activity but behind it there is a lost soul with nowhere to go but ever onwards towards self-negation.

All in all, compulsive helping is not the benign, innocent process that it might initially appear to be. It is as progressive and destructive as any other addiction.

Chapter Nine

Relationship Addiction

Compulsive helpers (who use themselves as drugs for other people) are directly mirrored by relationship addicts (who use other people as if they were drugs). Relationship addiction is a common cross-addiction with other forms of primary addictive behaviour. Alcoholics, drug addicts and people with eating disorders commonly also have a tendency towards forming addictive relationships. In these, the other individual is interchangeable with a bottle of whisky or a joint of cannabis or a slice of cake. The importance of the relationship is not the individual concerned but the emotional effect. Thus, for example, a sex and love addict would have no great interest in the other individual but solely in what can be taken from the relationship. The stimulant or soothing effect of the relationship may be no different from the stimulating or soothing effect of an addictive substance.

Addictive relationships are just as progressive and destructive as any other addiction. They can leave a trail of destruction behind them, just as any addictive process can be observed from the destruction left in its wake. We may not see the elephant but we can see where it has been and can deduce that only an elephant could cause so much damage.

As mentioned in chapter three, addictive relationships can be either dominant (threatening to harm the other person) or submissive (threatening to harm self). Both are forms of emotional blackmail and both avoid the openness and honesty necessary in any healthy relationship. Some individuals may have both dominant and submissive addictive relationships, sometimes at different times with the same person or, more commonly, in either dominant or submissive manner in different relationships. This mix is of no great clinical significance other than to demonstrate that one needs to fill in both questionnaires for relationship addiction, the dominant and the submissive, in order to get an accurate diagnosis. The addictive process is the same in general principle and the treatment, in due course, is also the same.

Also as illustrated in chapter three, compulsive helping can be divided into dominant and submissive tendencies. Compulsive helpers also can have primarily one or the other tendency, dominant or submissive, or sometimes both, either within one relationship or separately in different relationships. As with relationship addicts, there is no great clinical significance to this other than to ensure accurate diagnosis through filling in both compulsive helping questionnaires. The clinical outcome of dominant or submissive tendencies in compulsive helping is much the same and, in due course, the treatment is the same.

It is no great significance when one type of relationship addict (dominant or submissive) meets another type of compulsive helper (dominant and/or submissive). Whatever the particular combination, the result will be progressive and destructive as the addictive tendencies distort any possibility of a normal healthy relationship. What matters is the recognition that the relationship is addictive in nature, rather than precisely which type or combination of addictive relationship might be present. *All* addictive relationships are pathological. They are all unhealthy. They all bring misery in one form or another.

In simple terms, one can discover whether one is enmeshed in an addictive relationship of some kind or other by asking oneself what one gets from it. If the relationship brings constant stress and recrimination, subterfuge and suspicion, domination and sacrifice, then the probability is that the relationship is between two addicts or between an addict and a compulsive helper. Relationships between two compulsive helpers are rare; they tend to find each other's help exasperating. Of course it could happen that all this mayhem might occur in a non-addictive relationship, just as one can get unemployment, physical abuse, legal difficulties and physical problems in someone who is *not* alcoholic and who has no other form of primary addiction.

However, it is simply more probable that all these difficulties in combination will occur in an addict of some kind and it is more probable that all those relationship difficulties in combination will occur in an addictive relationship. Sometimes one can make a reasonable assumption that an elephant has passed by when one can see the particular form of widespread destruction that was caused on its travels.

For a compulsive helper, the easiest self-diagnosis of involvement in an addictive relationship is through an awareness that one is on a crusade, virtuous and healing, giving and not counting the cost. The idea that one *should* give and not count the cost is very strange. It devalues what one has to give. It offers something of one's own, regardless of whether the recipient will benefit or whether one will be left with anything for oneself or that one could use again another day. It is fascinating to see how many of these dangerous platitudes – such as "to give and not to count the cost" – have become ingrained in our culture. Compulsive helping, along with addictive relationships in general, takes a lot of rooting out.

Chapter Ten

Co-dependency

Co-dependency would be a perfectly reasonable term to describe the relationship between an addict and a compulsive helper. Unfortunately it has a great many other meanings:

Co-dependency on both alcohol and drugs.

Co-dependency on alcohol, drugs and people.

Co-dependency as a result of being abused or abandoned in childhood.

Co-dependency because one is in a relationship with an addict.

And so on and so on.

Most of all, co-dependency becomes an excuse: a reason to blame someone else – most commonly parents – for one's own problems. By contrast, the term "compulsive helping" blames nobody: it is simply a statement of acknowledgement, as for alcoholism or drug addiction. There is no saying where it came from, just an acknowledgement that one has it.

Unfortunately, the term "co-dependency" is so firmly established, in the literature as well as in the folklore of addiction, that it is probably impossible now to give it the full discredit that it deserves. Perhaps the best we can hope for is that its use will in time be restricted to the relationship between an addict and a compulsive helper.

The most bizarre and unacceptable use of the term "co-dependency" is when it is allied to "multi-generational shame". In this condition, co-dependency is said to be the product of the shame felt by an individual as a result of abuse or abandonment in childhood: as a result of that shame, the individual develops "co-dependency". This mysterious condition is given no precise symptoms and there is no way that it can be measured. All one can do is to observe the inevitability of the co-dependency subsequently developing into active addiction of one kind or another. Then it gets worse: it is transferred to the next generation when the co-dependent addictive individual has children and abuses or abandons them. In this way the next generation are shamed and become mysteriously co-dependent. Evidently the way to interfere with this progression of shame and co-dependency, from one generation to another, is to stop the abuse and abandonment.

This theoretical model is immensely popular, for the obvious reason that it blames parents or other people for the addict's behaviour. This is not to say that parents and others are always blameless. The sad fact is that childhood abuse and abandonment of one kind or another are extremely common, particularly in addictive families. Dysfunction of one kind or another is common in addictive families, and the children inevitably suffer as a result of this. However, this does not imply that the children will necessarily become addicts as a result of the family dysfunction or early childhood abuse and abandonment. Many children in addictive families have perfectly dreadful childhoods and yet grow up with no sign of addiction of any kind or even of compulsive helping. One can see this in many addictive families; there are children who survived anything and everything that was thrown at them. They had just as much abuse and abandonment and general dysfunction in their childhoods as their siblings. They grew up in the same environment and they had the same parents – but they inherited a different set of genes from those parents. The genes for primary addiction and compulsive helping passed them by.

The reason that there is such a high incidence of sex and love addiction in the children of sex and love addicts is therefore more likely to be because of genetic inheritance than simply as a direct repetition of learned behaviour or a product of consequential low self-esteem. Certainly learned behaviour may play a part, just as alcoholism is common in the children of alcoholic parents, probably as a result of familiarity with alcohol in the childhood environment. However, this does not mean that the alcoholism itself or any other specific form of addictive or compulsive behaviour, rather than a general addictive tendency, was transmitted from one generation to the next through genetic inheritance. Many children from alcoholic families develop other addictive outlets. Similarly, many children from sex and love-addicted parents develop other addictive tendencies. They do not inevitably become sex and love addicts even when they develop an addictive tendency of their own. Many develop no addictive tendency whatever.

The significance of these observations can be seen when the idea of abuse and abandonment leading to co-dependency and subsequent addiction does *not* work out in practice. It is now a full generation since these facile ideas were first preached. (The fervour of their adherents has a lot in common with that of revivalist preachers.) The addicts who welcomed these ideas with open arms – and blamed their parents and other people for making them into addicts – are now finding that they have addicted children of their own, even though they did not abuse or abandon them in any way. This could have been predicted from adoption studies but it shows just how fervently an obviously inaccurate perception will be believed when there is an opportunity to apportion blame to someone else rather than self.

There is no blame in the inheritance of addiction any more than there is blame in the inheritance of short sight. It is just the way that some of us are made. Without a doubt, parents *are* responsible for all sorts of dreadful things that are done to children. Abuse and abandonment *do* occur with distressing frequency. But they still do not *cause* addiction. They cause all sorts of other problems in emotional life and the children who have been abused or abandoned often require a very great deal of help, particularly when they come to make adult relationships of their own.

The emphasis that addiction does *not* come as a result of abuse or abandonment in childhood is extremely important when it comes to considering what treatment would be appropriate for addiction. If one believes it to be a product of abuse and abandonment, then psychotherapy of one kind or another should be effective in removing the emotional taint. However, if addiction is genetically inherited, then it has to be accepted and dealt with on a continuing day-to-day basis through working the Twelve Step programme of an Anonymous Fellowship such as Alcoholics Anonymous. Its active expression can be put into remission but the underlying tendency will persist. Each and every addict has to take responsibility for dealing with their own addiction, irrespective of what form of abuse or abandonment they may have experienced from parents or other people in childhood.

Co-dependents Anonymous (CoDA) and Adult Children of Alcoholics (ACOA) form the basis of their programme on the examination of someone else's behaviour. This is surely against the fundamental principles of a Twelve Step programme in which one has to acknowledge one's own dependency. By saying that one has been *made* co-dependent as a result of abuse or abandonment, or that one still suffers in adulthood from the effects of alcoholism in a parent, perpetuates the feelings of blame and self-pity that are at the core of all addictive behaviour. Surely one needs to move on from that. One needs first to acknowledge the truth of the abuse and abandonment rather than deny its existence, then acknowledge that it was wrong and that one did not deserve it – and then move on.

Ageing Well by George Vaillant (Little, Brown 2002) gives the fascinating story of fifty years of follow-up of three large cohorts of individuals recruited in their youth into a study by Harvard University. It shows conclusively that some people have remarkable powers of survival when they have a mind to employ them, whereas other people who choose to wallow in misery will do so for the rest of their lives, despite having had no worse experiences in childhood than those who age well. CoDA and ACOA may inadvertently perpetuate self-pity and blame rather than help addicts towards mature acceptance of their own responsibilities, irrespective of whatever may have been done to them in the past. The term "co-dependency" when used carelessly, has a lot to answer for.

Chapter Eleven

People Pleasing

People-pleasing – doing what one thinks will please other people even though one might not want to do it – is a fraudulent behaviour. It is usually employed because one wants to get something back in return. It is manipulative and dishonest. It can be employed by anybody, addicts or otherwise. Obviously addicts, people with neurotransmission disease, are highly manipulative, they learn that skill in earliest childhood and they become expert people-pleasers. However, people-pleasing is an acquired behavioural trait rather than something that is genetically inherited. By contrast, compulsive helping probably is genetically inherited.

There are six characteristics that can be identified in early childhood that might indicate that a particular child is likely to develop an addictive tendency as he or she gets older:

i.   Coming from an addictive family. (One should look for a family history of eating disorders, nicotine addiction, prescription drug addiction and compulsive gambling and other addictive tendencies rather than simply alcoholism and recreational drug addiction.)

ii. The tendency to be emotionally isolated, even when surrounded by friends or even when "acting out" in a flamboyant manner.

iii. The tendency to have wild mood swings irrespective of circumstance. (There may be no obvious reason for the child being elated one moment or depressed the next.)

iv. Being highly manipulative. (All children are manipulative but addictive children have particular skills in this respect.)

v.   The tendency to be very fragile emotionally. (These children are very easily hurt even though they may superficially appear to be tough.)

vi. The tendency to be easily frustrated. (The attention span may be short and nothing ever seems to satisfy.)

Having three or four of these characteristics would be a significant pointer towards the development of addictive tendencies in later life. At present this observation is no more than an educated guess, based primarily upon retrospective analysis – working backwards from the adult situation – and this can be notoriously inaccurate. Even so, these characteristics are well worth examining because of the sheer significance of the possibility of early diagnosis. If one can identify a potentially addictive child *before* the use of alcohol or drugs or other addictive substances or processes, then hopefully one can do something about steering that child towards abstinence and towards working a preventive Twelve Step programme. Hopefully, one can guide the child towards making honest relationships rather than those that are manipulative or dishonest in other ways. Even more importantly, the correct diagnosis – having an addictive potential – should prevent the common inappropriate diagnosis of Attention Deficit Hyperactivity Disorder. In this condition the diagnosis of the child appeases the parent. Behavioural problems and school failure can be blamed on a clinical condition and then treated with drugs. Medicalising the behaviour normalises it.

Interestingly, that same accusation of medicalising a behavioural problem is often laid at the door of Twelve Step treatment programmes when they refer to addictive "disease". The crucial difference is in the treatment: the Twelve Step programme uses behavioural rather than medicinal approaches. A diagnosis of depression in children with the potential for addiction would be correct but it does not follow that it should be treated with anti-depressants. In future years the current use of amphetamines for children with Attention Deficit Hyperactivity Disorder and anti-depressants for children who have mood disturbances will be seen to be one of the great clinical scandals of all time. Young developing brain tissue is swamped with drugs; developing minds are given chemical and psychological dependencies. This cannot be right in any circumstances. It is a disgrace.

In this respect "people-pleasing" refers to the behaviour of the doctor in prescribing for the child in order to give the parent an acceptable diagnosis and a form of treatment that takes away all responsibility from the parent for the child's behaviour. The term "potential addict" should also take some responsibility away from the parents for the behaviour of the child – but the current acceptance of addictive behaviour as a genetically inherited "dis-ease" is not yet at a level at which most parents are likely to be grateful for that diagnosis.

- People-pleasing is commonplace in medical practice. Patients crave a diagnosis – particularly in the emotional field – that excuses them from personal responsibility for their condition. Thus "depression" is acceptable whereas "inadequate sense of personal responsibility" might be accurate in some patients but would certainly not be well received by them as a diagnosis. Doctors, being human, will tend to people-please and give patients the diagnoses that they want. Unfortunately this then often leads to giving the treatment that people want. However much doctors may be criticised for over-prescribing, there is none the less a collusion between patients and their doctors in this respect, especially in the use of mood-altering pharmaceutical drugs. In the UK over forty million prescriptions are written each year for anti-depressants, tranquillisers or sleeping tablets, drugs that act on the mind. This level of prescribing cannot possibly be *necessary*, even when disguised as "help" and when doctors claim that they have no time to do other than prescribe. But the supplicant patient often goes away satisfied, particularly when the taking of each and every tablet is accompanied by the self-talk "I am sick. I am not responsible". To spend time with patients is more challenging but, interestingly, the offer is often declined by the patients. Some are perfectly happy with their symptoms, precisely because they enable the doctor and patient to medicalise them. People-pleasing by doctors can therefore have significant pharmacological consequences and be a very unhealthy process indeed.

- People-pleasing by teachers often results in them refusing to assess pupils in a measurable way. The fear of "elitism" is bizarre. Families and, in due course, employers have every reason to want to know what the school system can actually achieve. One may not necessarily value academic achievement above all else but it does at least give some yardstick by which to measure particular ability. I personally value my own associateship of the Royal College of Music, in a performer's diploma, because I know how hard I had to work for it and because it demonstrated a practical skill that I once possessed. I am less proud of my medical qualifications because I believe that they say no more than that I was bright enough to get into medical school and therefore should be bright enough to come out at the other end with a degree. Even so, I believe that doctors do have to be set examinations because we have to be able to demonstrate our competence before we are let loose on patients. For teachers or educationalists to denigrate all examinations is therefore totally inappropriate.

- For lawyers, and senior judges in particular, to make out that punishments should vary according to the social circumstance of the perpetrator rather than on an absolute scale of legality or illegality, is equally bizarre. One can temper justice with mercy but utter confusion reigns when the law itself can be bent to suit political or sociological perceptions.

- Politicians are very often the ultimate people-pleasers, for ever making promises that they know they cannot keep. I once asked the Director of Social Services of a local borough if he could tell me what percentage of the problems that he was required by law to alleviate he could meet within his budget, when taking account of the human resources available and the number of hours in a working day. Two weeks later he returned with the shocked realisation; "Less than 5%". He could not possibly deliver the services that politicians expected of him. We ourselves come to expect our politicians to "lie" in this respect. If the truth be known, we want to get them to nurture our own sacred cows but ignore those of other people. We want budgets to be infinite, yet applied locally and precisely as we would wish. We *expect* our politicians to be people-pleasers.

In each of these professional examples, for doctors, teachers, lawyers and politicians, the product of people-pleasing – saying and doing what people want to hear or receive – can be very destructive indeed. Addicts and compulsive helpers are not the only people in the world who cause problems.

Chapter Twelve

Selflessness

Selflessness can be taken to extremes. Surely each one of us is entitled to make the best of our lives, provided that we do not do so at the expense of other people. We have a right to our place on the planet, a right to be treated with courtesy and respect, a right to be heard and for our viewpoints to be considered. Further, if we want this for ourselves, we should want other people to have these same things. To deny one's own rights can imply that one denies other people's rights as well. Only by respecting and valuing ourselves can we develop equal respect and concern for the value of other people's individuality. When we treat ourselves as worthless, or as just a number, we would risk doing the same to other people. In this respect, being selfless – having no true sense of one's own value – can lead to one's having no true sense of the value of other people. That leads to the concentration camps.

It is only when we have a true sense of value of ourselves, valuing our own ideas and our own right to put them into practice, that we fight for these same freedoms for other people. When truly valuing ourselves, we value others as well. I may consider that I have rights but, in doing so, I have to respect yours. If I value myself I must also value you.

The sense of self, of self-image, is therefore vitally important individually and socially. Addictive disease is very much a disease of self-image. Depression and addiction are really the same thing, before and after "treatment" with various mood-altering substances or processes, be they legal, illegal, prescribed, normally used as a food or even, in the case of work or exercise, considered to be healthy. In each case, however, addicts will use them unhealthily, becoming dependent upon them in order to feel good about themselves. Inevitably this false "high" wears off and leads to a crashing "low", which sets up the need for the next use of the mood-altering substance or process.

However hard addicts protest and say that they are just doing what everybody else does and that they are not really addicted, they know perfectly well that things are not right. Their dependency illustrates that all the razzamatazz of their lives is merely a false front, papering over a deep sense of inner emptiness. The acquisition of self-esteem may become tied into acquisition of material things or the fickle friendships that go with life in the fast lane. People who are depressed or addicted may try to nurture themselves with simple rewards that they consider would not be particularly harmful, certainly not to anyone else but themselves. Or they may bury themselves in relationships, searching for true love, or at least for some form of comfort or sense of significance. All these desperate attempts to find temporary respite from the underlying mood disorder are doomed to failure. They are not based upon anything substantial. A drunken binge is followed by a hangover, a spending spree by an irritated bank manager and concerned husband or wife, starving and purging by the realisation that the sense of relief is very short-lived, the amazing new relationship by the discovery that it provided no more security or warmth than the last one. Self-esteem gets progressively lower as the depression or addiction progresses.

For compulsive helpers, the need to be needed becomes a whip for the back, a cross to bear, a path towards destruction through dedication. The self-esteem of the compulsive helper is obtained largely through service for other people. The compulsive helper always has to be *doing* something. There is no natural calm or contentment, only worthy work. In this way selflessness negates individual life. There is nothing left of the personal identity other than a roll-call of achievements in the service of others. This is not to denigrate service for others but it is to say that service to self should have an equivalent place. The exhortation to treat others AS oneself quite specifically does not say "better than". There is good reason for that. Ultimately putting oneself at the bottom of the pile creates either a resentment towards other people or a progressive destruction of one's own self-esteem. The newspapers – and public folklore in general – make saints out of people who sacrifice themselves in the service of others. That cannot be right. Life must have more individual significance. Surely the true benefactors of society are those who create and build things, set up industries and devise management and marketing systems in order to stimulate the economy. These are the very people who are most commonly denigrated as being selfish and self-serving. While stimulating the economy upon which everyone else depends, they are designated as "fat cats" and thought to be parasitic upon their workforce whereas in fact they lead them and provide for them by creating the opportunities for employment.

When the state becomes the employer, it has to be subsidised by the private industrialist. How strange it is that our society sanctifies the self-destructive and dependent while demonising the self-enhancing and creative!

To retreat from the world of commerce, trade, manufacturing and the service sector is to retreat from reality. Eco-warriors live in a dream world, a fanciful and superficially charming world that would be an absolute nightmare if one had to live in it for any length of time. The Middle Ages were not "the good old days" by any stretch of the imagination; yet that is precisely where the eco-warriors would lead us in their anti-industrialisation. Their intentions may be benign but the ultimate consequences of putting their ideas into practice would be savage.

Exactly that same principle holds true for compulsive helpers. They may wish nothing but good for the world, but what they achieve in practice is often the very opposite. By being selfless, they retreat from the responsibility of stating a personal opinion and standing by it. By doing things for other people rather than for themselves they contribute to totalitarian ideas, in which we all belong to the state or the church and have to do the will of their leaders. The only protection against that dreadful fate is individualism, valuing each individual *as* an individual and for what he or she can produce (if he or she is physically and mentally able to do so), not specifically for the benefit of others but for the benefit of self. This apparent paradox is explained by the fact that people who generate things for themselves do inevitably generate things for other people in the process. Conversely, people who focus on the needs of others are often very poor at actually creating things and may rely upon others for that.

This picture of the compulsive helper as being dedicated to the lives of others, but relying upon someone else to produce the basic resources, is common but not universal. Another form of compulsive helper is the rather sad figure who is highly creative and industrious but who has bought into the idea that this is unworthy; that the true creators of society are not the industrialists but the doctors and teachers, artists and playwrights. These compulsive helpers donate huge amounts of time, energy and money to establishing and running medical and educational institutions and sponsoring the arts. The recipients of their gifts very often scorn them. Doctors and teachers may believe that they really are doing "good" work simply because they believe that they are caring for other people or educating them. Sometimes this "good" (virtuous) work can be thoroughly "bad" (incompetent). These professionals, when working in the state sector, may take their salaries for granted, rarely giving a thought to the people who produce the wealth that they are only too eager to take and spend. The artists and playwrights go further, often producing works that are deliberately critical of people in the commercial and industrial world – the very people who support them financially.

It is unhealthy for society to be able to get away with biting the hand that feeds it. Adolescents have to be taught the basic realities of home life; they have to learn to be considerate of others and they have to contribute something in return for what they receive. They certainly have to learn those same lessons pretty quickly when they get a job in the private sector or when they get married and have children. Compulsive helpers set a very poor example in this respect by bailing out adolescents (of all ages) from the consequences of their intolerant and destructive behaviour. In this way compulsive helping is *not* a force for good; it can cause a great deal of harm.

Chapter Thirteen

Does Compulsive Helping Actually Help?

The last person I would want as a lover is a sex and love addict. I don't want to be an object: I want to be me. The last person I would want as an employee is a workaholic. I want someone who does the job well, not people who drive themself into the ground and achieve an enormous amount one day but nothing whatever for the next two. The last person I want to look after me is a compulsive helper. I want someone to provide genuine help rather than to fuss and bother over me. I want someone who has sound judgement rather than fervent beliefs in the correctness of his or her own vision. I want someone who respects my rights to make my own mistakes and learn from my own experience.

Set in this light, alongside other addictive tendencies, compulsive helping can be seen to be potentially just as destructive as any other addictive or compulsive behaviour.

"Help" is a fascinating subject because true help is very often the opposite of what might first appear to be helpful. We all know the example of doing the child's homework. When the teacher adds the initials W.D.M. (Well Done Mum!) we can see the true effects of the compulsive helper; the teacher knew perfectly well that the child did not have the knowledge or the skills to produce such accurate homework. The mother did not help the child by doing the homework. At best she might have been trying to instil confidence and self-esteem through obtaining a higher mark than the child would otherwise have obtained. But the child will have known perfectly well – as did the teacher – that this was not his or her own work. The high mark would have been unearned and therefore very damaging to self-esteem. A teacher who was less aware of the ambitions of compulsive helper parents, might have believed the high mark and given great credit to the child, forcing his or her self-esteem even lower. Furthermore, if the child comes to believe that all life's difficulties can be solved by getting someone else to do the tricky bit, then the compulsive helping mother will have set in motion a very destructive train of future expectations associated with emotional immaturity and lack of personal responsibility.

The international aid agencies know only too well, from practical experience, that giving money may fuel corruption, idleness and the expectation of more. Giving goods or subsidies may destroy the local economy. Giving undeserved patronage may produce personal conceit and lead to poor productivity and unreal expectations for the future. The aid agencies have learnt to train and develop skills so that people are best able to help themselves.

When doctors do too much for their patients, they create a dependency. When they give a pill for every ill, the patient comes to expect magical solutions for all life's problems and then becomes bitterly resentful when they don't work. When surgeons believe that all life's problems can be solved through the knife, they may damage and mutilate. They may believe that they are doing good when they wire the jaws together for a compulsive overeater or when they staple the stomach or shorten the intestine. All these are physical attempts to treat an emotional problem that will inevitably recur unless the underlying psychological problem is addressed. When a psychoanalyst spends years indoctrinating his or her subject, the end result may be little more than a zombie who has learned to recite the jargon and blame parents for all life's problems.

When politicians exalt the poor and the needy, the sick and the underprivileged, the weak and the downtrodden, they may at times be providing succour to the incompetent or lazy, the inadequate or even the unprincipled.

In each of these examples, compulsive helpers in these various professions can do too much. They may lose any sense of true judgement. They focus upon need rather than potential. They provide rationalisations, excuses and justifications rather than sound, impartial appraisal. They have axes to grind and may never see the harm that they are doing.

The most helpful things that a compulsive helper might learn to say are:

- "I do not accept this behaviour in my home. I want a better relationship with you than your behaviour offers me."

- "I am not prepared to carry you and your difficulties at work. If you have problems, then seek help or do something about them rather than expect me for ever to pick up the pieces."

- "If you have debts then ask yourself how you got them. Everybody has credit cards but only you spent your money in the way that you did."

- "No, I am not going to tell you the answer. Work it out for yourself."

- "Why should I give you money? Earn your own. You are perfectly capable of doing so."

- "Why should the state pay for you? You have responsibilities as well as rights."

- "Why should you receive a subsidy or grant? Why should your activity be valued outside the commercial marketplace?"

- "No, I do not consider the fact that you were drunk to be an excuse for your behaviour; it compounds it."

- "No I am not going to tell a lie to your teacher; the dog did not eat your homework – you didn't do it."

- "No I am not going to prescribe anti-depressants. I do not believe that they would be helpful. They would simply take away your capacity to work out solutions that would be more helpful in the long term. Anti-depressants would disguise the need for a different personal philosophy."

- "No, I shall not vote for that in Parliament. I do not believe in it. I think for myself. I am not merely the rubber stamp of party activists in the constituency."

All these things are very difficult to say. They demand courage and self-confidence. They involve taking a risk, knowing that there could be dire consequences. Indeed, that is precisely the point; each of these statements illustrates when blackmail is *not* being paid.

Compulsive helpers pay the addict's blackmail time and time again. They do so willingly, in the belief that they really are helping. When the problems are not solved by their help, they blame themselves, thinking that they didn't understand the problem correctly or that they should have tried harder or done something differently. In each case, they find a justification for carrying on with their compulsive helping, rather than examining it to see its moral deficiencies and failure in practical end-results. In particular, when confronting addictive behaviour, compulsive helpers need to learn to make a point and stick to it. Addicts are expert manipulators and can quite happily change sides in the middle of an argument. To hold one's own ground in the face of such an onslaught requires a very clear sense of self and a firm belief in the right to one's own viewpoints. Compulsive helpers find that exceedingly difficult but it is what has to be done.

The *folie à deux* between the addict and the compulsive helper is as progressive and destructive as are the individual addictive processes of primary addiction or compulsive helping. Not only does each individual get progressively worse, the relationship between them becomes progressively more enmeshed and dysfunctional. The increasing demands for "the need to be fixed" get progressively more tied up with the increasing demands for "the need to be needed". Boundaries are ignored and finally lost altogether. The relationship becomes all-absorbing, an alien parasite preying upon the lives of both individuals. In this final degraded state, both the addict and the compulsive helper have a responsibility to withdraw from the madness of the relationship and take care of themselves rather than continue their destructive dependency upon each other.

Chapter Fourteen

Confrontation

There is only one thing that motivates addicts to change their behaviour; pain. To be precise, it is the painful perception that continuing as they are will be more painful than giving up their addictive substances or processes. This pain is far more than the physical and psychological pain of withdrawal; it is the prospect of being without the immediate "treatment" for all life's problems. Doing without their long-term "anti-depressants" implies to them that they will go back into the depressive pit.

This fear is understandable and the prospect of having to endure it is very painful. On the other hand, continuing addictive behaviour results in cumulative damage right across the whole spectrum of human experience. There is no other condition – cancer, heart disease, diabetes, unemployment, bereavement – that causes such widespread damage as addictive or compulsive behaviour. It affects the whole range of human experience. There are damaging consequences economically, professionally, maritally, socially, medically, legally, intellectually, everywhere. In time these damaging consequences become increasingly painful to the addict. This results in the classic dilemma, to continue and therefore get more damaging consequences, or to give up and return to the sense of inner emptiness and despair. At both extremes, life loses its point. Addicts often realise this and therefore commit suicide. The Samaritans estimate that between 30% and 40% of all suicides occur in alcoholics. Adding in drug addicts and eating disorder sufferers, compulsive gamblers and the rest, it can be seen that the majority of suicides are people afflicted by addictive or compulsive behaviour.

Into this breech step the compulsive helpers, determined to do what they can to "help" the addicts. They recognise the inner emptiness and despair and the risk of suicide, and they try to make life easier. They do this by reducing the painful consequences of addictive behaviour:

- They pay off the debts.

- They take on more work.

- They tidy up the social damage or reduce social contact so that less damage occurs in future.

- They pay fines and employ lawyers.

- They talk and talk for hour after hour, pleading, explaining, discussing, making plans, writing lists, preparing budgets, finding experts, reading articles and books, doing everything they possibly can to find solutions to all the problems that the addicts create. Meanwhile the addicts continue exactly as they did before. Why on earth would they ever need to change while the compulsive helpers are doing all the work and taking all the worry?

In our society it goes against the grain to leave people in pain. We help people when they have 'flu, we administer first aid after accidents, we try to resuscitate people when they have heart attacks, we visit them when they are in hospital and we see what we can do to help at home or at work when, for one reason or another, they are unable to look after themselves. For family members and friends we go even further, especially if they are addicts. We spend money and time, taking risks and doing all sorts of things in the hope that something will help. Each new tiny glimpse of hope is greeted with untold joy and effusive encouragement. The subsequent disappointment resulting from further relapse is born stoically – and then the whole process starts all over again.

If only compulsive helpers would keep a set of notes on their beliefs and actions, and the consequences of their interventions, they might then see earlier than otherwise that their behaviour makes things worse for the addict rather than better. Against all of our cultural upbringing, addicts do *not* benefit from being "helped" in traditional ways. They need to be confronted over their behaviour and have the damaging consequences spelt out to them very clearly – and not be allowed to make excuses, justifications and rationalisations.

Perhaps the most stark contrast between the good intentions of compulsive helpers and the cynicism of addicts is seen in the question "What's green and gets you high?", to which the addict answers "A social security giro cheque". The purpose of social security money is to provide food and clothing and other basic necessities of life. For the addict the drugs, or other mood-altering substances and processes, *are* the necessities.

Perhaps, in the worst example of all, compulsive helping by officialdom is seen in Methadone maintenance programmes and needle exchange systems for heroin addicts. Methadone (Physeptone) is a liquid that is prescribed as an alternative to injectable heroin. In this way it is hoped that the incidence of hepatitis B and C and AIDS will be reduced, that there will be a smaller risk of these conditions being spread into the general heterosexual population via needle-using addicts working as prostitutes, and that crime will be reduced when addicts no longer need to use illegal methods to get their supply of drugs. The needle exchange systems take it for granted that addicts will continue to use drugs but it is hoped that the medical consequences of their doing so will be reduced. The theory looks fine; the practice is an absolute disaster.

A study by *The Big Issue* in Manchester found that 50% of addicts on Methadone maintenance programmes were using *daily* heroin in addition to their legal supply of "medicinal" Methadone. The remainder were commonly using illegal drugs on a less frequent basis. In other words, the prescription of a "safe" alternative was not safe at all; the addicts used it in addition to heroin rather than as an alternative. The medical risks continued. Crime continued. Furthermore, Methadone prescriptions were often sold on the black market because some addicts found that they actually preferred it to heroin. Even more dangerously, young people were sometimes introduced to opiates via medicinally-prescribed Methadone, bought on the black market, because they believed a prescription drug must necessarily be relatively safe.

All this could have been predicted if the powers that be had simply asked themselves the question, "What would happen if we gave four pints of beer a day to an alcoholic?". Everyone knows the answer to that; the alcoholic would say "Thank you" and see those four pints of beer as a daily starter, rather than as an alternative to further drinking. The Department of Health has a great deal to answer for in its failure to recognise the common ground between alcoholism and drug addiction, let alone nicotine addiction, eating disorders, compulsive gambling and other forms of addictive or compulsive behaviour. By seeing alcoholism as the product of drinking too much alcohol or as the rather sad consequences of moral decay or social disaster, rather than as an illness that is probably genetically inherited, the Department of Health – and many doctors – completely fail to identify alcoholism at an early stage and hence fail to provide appropriate treatment. By seeing drug addiction as a depravity, or as the unfortunate consequence of poor social environment or youthful experiment, they fail to differentiate between addictive disease and stupidity.

Again this diagnostic failure has devastating consequences. Addicts who could be helped are left to rot. In the National Health Service more than a million prescriptions are now written each year for Methadone. This is a terrible indictment of the medical profession's willingness to write off a sector of the population by failing to see that they have an illness that can be helped. The Methadone that they prescribe now kills as many people as those who died through taking heroin. Any other medicinal treatment associated with such a devastating outcome would be banned instantly. Imagine what would happen if a brand of insulin was found to kill as many people suffering from diabetes as would have died from the untreated condition! The Department of Health writes off addicts. So, generally, do doctors. Medical schools do not teach the non-medicinal treatment of addiction through a Twelve Step programme. In the UK there are two thousand four hundred groups of Alcoholics Anonymous meeting every week and yet the ideas are still not taught in medical school.

The Department of Health recently funded a massive survey designed to demonstrate that alcoholics could go back to "sensible" drinking. What possible advantage could there be from that study? Why would someone who has suffered so much – along with the family and everyone else associated with an alcoholic – *want* to go back to sensible drinking? Does alcohol really occupy such a central part of our social life, let alone economic life for the government, that it is seen as a necessity and that abstinence is seen as a tragedy? One would have hoped that the doctors in the Department of Health, of all people, would have known the catastrophic medical consequences of alcoholism:

- One in five of all hospital beds is occupied by somebody with alcohol-related conditions.

- One hundred people a day die from the consequences of their alcohol consumption, in contrast to fifteen people a day from all the illegal drugs put together.

- One in two of all people seen in hospital Accident and Emergency Departments is there as a result of the use of either alcohol or drugs.

- Ten per cent of all post mortems show evidence of serious liver damage from alcohol.

- Eighty-five per cent of domestic violence incidents are associated with the use of alcohol.

- Thirty to forty per cent of all suicides are in alcoholics.

Faced with this evidence, the British Medical Association (BMA) has its own wine club and campaigns against professional boxing but not against rugby football, rock climbing or horse riding which are undertaken equally voluntarily and which cause many more fatalities and serious injuries. I am no prohibitionist – quite the reverse, I am a libertarian – but I believe that the priorities of the BMA leave a lot to be desired.

The general medical understanding of eating disorders is equally inadequate. Anorexia tends to be seen as a distinct psychiatric condition rather than as part of the spectrum of addictive and compulsive behaviour. Bulimia tends to be seen as a rather sad consequence of a mis-placed dedication to fashion and hence to a particular body weight or shape. Compulsive overeating is not seen at all as an addictive process, although precisely how people come to be massively obese without having been overeaters does not appear to be considered. Obesity cannot simply have occurred overnight.

The medical profession is equally reluctant to face up to the addictive nature of various prescription medications. I recall a professor of psychiatry telling me thirty years ago that he prescribed barbiturates to help people sleep and amphetamines to wake them up again in the morning and that he knew that he could do so safely because neither substance was addictive. Our understanding has changed with time but only slowly and with great resistance. The fight to get benzodiazepines (Diazepam, Lorazepam etc.) recognised as addictive drugs was long and the defensive resistance was considerable. The fight to prove that anti-depressants are addictive – as they must be, simply as a result of their mood-altering properties, even though they take weeks rather than days or minutes to take effect or produce withdrawal symptoms – is still being fought. There is a very simple reason for this;

in six years of medical school training I had not one single lesson on human psychology or on counselling, yet I had years of training in pharmacology and therapeutics. I agree that it is sensible for trainee doctors to spend time on pharmacology and therapeutics – because we are the only people licensed to prescribe medications – but we should not do this to the *total* exclusion of training in human psychology and in counselling skills.

The philosophical ideas that underpin the National Health Service – that resources should be distributed according to need (rather than in accordance with the capacity of the recipient to benefit), that resources should be distributed at the time of need (rather than requiring that people should make some provision for their own immediate care in the same way as they make provision for food and clothing) and that the state should ultimately take responsibility for the individual (thus creating a dependency culture) are at the heart of the failure to tackle addiction, the greatest scourge of our time. All the major clinical conditions such as heart attacks, strokes, chronic bronchitis and emphysema, cancer, stomach ulcers, liver disease, accidents, AIDS, hepatitis B and C, the various consequences of obesity and many more – are very commonly related to alcoholism, drug addiction, nicotine addiction, eating disorders and other forms of addictive or compulsive behaviour. We do not help patients by treating only the consequences of their addictive or compulsive behaviour rather than trying to tackle it at source. Yet in medical school I was given not one single lesson on addiction as such, only repeated training on how to treat its consequences.

If we are to tackle addictive behaviour in our society, then we have to do far more than tackle the *supply* side through taxation on alcohol and nicotine and through the efforts of the police and customs officials to reduce the number of illegal drugs being brought into this country. We have to tackle the *demand* side; the reason why people want to use mood-altering substances and behaviours in the first place. We also have to be able to identify that proportion of the population (probably about ten per cent) who have addictive tendencies, we have to educate them appropriately from primary school onwards and we have to give painful consequences to their addictive or compulsive behaviour, rather than bale them out.

The theory is obvious but the practical implementation is exceedingly difficult. Are we to ignore cigarette smokers when they have heart attacks or develop cancer? Obviously not, but we could insist that the price of cigarettes should include the cost of treating these conditions and the cost of training doctors and nurses. If it is to be argued that we should reduce the tax on cigarettes because few smokers live to collect their pensions, we should also have to argue that blind people should not pay towards the cost of street-lighting – and so on. Should we remove social security support from drug addicts and should we abolish Methadone maintenance and needle exchange systems? Probably the answer to these questions should be "Yes". This may seem harsh, and it is. However, the world of addiction is harsh and sometimes we need harsh measures in order to treat harsh problems. I am not advocating that we should *cause* pain for addicts but rather that we should leave them in the pain that they cause themselves. This would be exceedingly difficult for governments and for doctors and other health workers, let alone for social workers whose whole lives are dedicated towards trying to reduce social problems. Yet my whole point is that we should totally support that goal; by leaving people with the consequences of their behaviour we will encourage them to change that behaviour whereas by taking away the consequences we collude with it. If more addicts end up in prison – it is already estimated that eighty per cent of the prison population have addiction problems of one kind or another – then all the more reason for establishing Twelve Step treatment programmes in all prisons.

I have spent much of my professional life helping people to give up addictive or compulsive behaviour of one kind or another and find appropriate behavioural alternatives. I do not prescribe drugs – anti-depressants or tranquillisers or sleeping tablets – to patients receiving counselling. On exactly the same basis I do not sit down to have a deep heart-felt conversation with someone who is drunk. There is no way into a mind that is under the influence of mood-altering substances or processes. Talking to a nicotine addict on the potential medical risks of cigarette-smoking is a complete waste of time. It does *not* change behaviour. Equally, trying to instil fear into drug addicts or alcoholics, or other people suffering from addictive or compulsive behaviour does *not* influence their behaviour. Fear is not a long-term effective motive. Only pain has that essential power.

I remember once giving evidence to the Social Services Committee of the House of Commons. On hearing my suggestions, one of the members of the committee said, "Dr Lefever, you appear to be wanting to turn the National Health Service upside down". I agreed that I was trying to do exactly that; I wanted to try to get it to focus upon prevention and upon helping people to be responsible, as far as possible, for themselves. These are unquestionably worthy goals – but their implementation within the National Health Service will take a very great deal of rethinking and alternative distribution of resources. Considering its myriad consequences, addiction is without doubt the major clinical problem of our time. We have to do something about it. Our current methods require to be completely rethought.

The first requirement is that compulsive helpers should be separated – kicking and screaming – from the treatment of addicts. At the individual level, compulsive helpers need to be shown that their methods of "helping" have the exact opposite result. Demonstrating that pocket money is being spent on cannabis or that paying off a fine simply perpetuates addictive behaviour, or that pouring alcohol down the sink simply results in it being hidden in future, or that taking on more work in order to make up for gambling losses simply results in the gambler carrying on gambling, will have some educational effect, particularly when this understanding is acquired in a group therapy setting where people can see each other's behaviour and thereby gain insight into their own.

In the macrocosm of medical practice, social work, the law and politics, the turn-around in understanding and in prescribed solutions for current social ills has to be profound. We are simply not going to solve today's problems with the solutions of today. We have to see that the welfare state now often achieves the very opposite of its intentions; it may sometimes perpetuate suffering rather than relieve it, it rewards irresponsibility and incompetence rather than thrift, enterprise and emotional maturity. Above all, we have to train people to understand that compulsive helping is a vice rather than a virtue.

Chapter Fifteen

True Help

I have spent my entire life in a helping profession. I want to be helpful. I was born into a family of professional helpers: teachers, clergy and politicians. My brother was the first lawyer in the family and I was the first doctor. All of us, one way or another, try to play our part in helping others. My wife Meg is a physiotherapist, teacher and counsellor and she works with me, in particular by running our family programmes at PROMIS.

In the private sector, in which the majority of our patients are referred to us by previous patients, we have had to learn very quickly which ideas work and which ideas do not, otherwise we would go out of business. We could have gone down the easy route of prescribing Methadone and anti-depressants but we did not choose that option in the treatment of our own son Robin's addiction (he now has a degree in psychology and is the director of the in-patient PROMIS Recovery Centre and out-patient PROMIS Counselling Centre) and we therefore do not believe that we should offer this non-treatment to anyone else.

At the in-patient PROMIS Recovery Centre in Nonington, near Canterbury in Kent, we have treated over three thousand five hundred people suffering from depression and all forms of addictive or compulsive behaviour over the last nineteen years. Professor Geoffrey Stephenson, Emeritus Professor of Psychology at the University of Kent at Canterbury, who oversees our outcome studies, found that sixty-five per cent of our patients were still abstinent, or significantly improved in various measures in their lives, one year after leaving treatment. This result was true for alcoholism, drug addiction and for bulimia and compulsive overeating whereas for anorexia the figure was only thirty per cent. However, our anorexic patients tended to be older and to have had more previous treatments than those in other studies performed elsewhere. It could therefore be said that we were helping thirty per cent of other people's failures. That figure is still desperately low and we have now established a separate eating disorder unit specifically in order to try to improve the outcome for this particular group of patients.

In London, in addition to our out-patient PROMIS Counselling Centre in South Kensington, we have established two halfway houses, extended care facilities in which patients live and have to provide their own food and generally look after themselves but from which they come to the PROMIS Counselling Centre for therapeutic support each day. Gradually, after beginning on a seven-day week, they progressively reduce their time with us so that they become more independent and return to employment, or go on training courses, so that they can in due course become independent. We discourage them from remaining dependent upon social security or parental or other support. Our intention is to help our patients to be free from all forms of dependency. We have found that the institution of these halfway houses has significantly reduced the relapse rate of patients in early recovery. As Geraldine O. Delaney, the legendary director of Little Hill, the treatment centre in Alina Lodge, New Jersey, USA (where she admitted patients only if they had been thrown out of three other treatment centres) said, "The most important ingredient of recovery is tincture of time". The longer we can help people to be free from addictive substances and processes, then the better will be their long-term chances of further full abstinence.

We find that one of the principal causes of relapse in early recovery is compulsive helping, either co-existent compulsive helping in the patients themselves, alongside their primary addictions, or compulsive helping by families. When the patient takes his or her mind off self, and goes on an individual crusade trying to help another addict, it is more probable that he or she will be pulled down rather than be able to help the other addict to be pulled up. We ourselves do not do one-to-one work as a general rule because we know that any patient's addictive disease will always have the potential to be stronger than our own recovery. We can be outwitted, bamboozled, manipulated and controlled, even though we have seen the whole repertoire of these behaviours many times before. We therefore tend to focus upon group therapy, using the strength of the group itself to support and confront its own members. We act as facilitators rather than primary helpers.

The mistake that family members sometimes make is to equate abstinence with recovery. Abstinence is merely the process of staying away from particular addictive substances or processes. Recovery is the full recognition that one is an addict by nature and that one therefore has to do various things on a day-to-day basis, and avoid others, in order to stay in continuing recovery. Just as someone with diabetes has to reduce carbohydrate foods and often has to take insulin or other medications, addicts have to avoid all mood-altering substances and processes (because these would tend to keep the addictive potential ticking over) and work the Twelve Step programme of the Anonymous Fellowships on a continuing basis. Only that way is abstinence maintained in the long term as a matter of course rather than in the short term with clenched fists and gritted teeth.

When family members make this mistake, confusing abstinence with recovery, they may take their eye off the ball, seeing what they want to see rather than what is actually happening. They may give lavish presents simply to commemorate the completion of treatment. This, in turn, takes the addict's eye off the ball so that he or she feels that treatment really achieved something more than being simply an educational process that enables him or her to start work in the real world and maintain recovery through working the Twelve Step programme in the Anonymous Fellowships.

We therefore encourage family members to continue coming to our family programme sessions even after the patient has left treatment. This process keeps them focused upon recognising the long-term risks of an addictive tendency rather than simply the short-term behaviour associated with active addiction. Correspondingly, we recommend the addicts themselves to attend regular aftercare sessions each week for up to two years. Most of all, in this way, they are supported by each other. This support is exactly what we hope to achieve rather than to get them dependent upon the counselling staff.

A great deal of damage can be caused when counselling staff are themselves compulsive helpers. Their professional work becomes a personal crusade. They become devastated when patients relapse, believing it to be a sign of their own professional failure. They tend to do too much for their patients rather than too little. They steer them towards further dependency rather than towards independence and self-reliance. Of course, addicts will lap this up and say that the compulsive helper counsellor is the best ever. At PROMIS we establish quite clearly in the Counsellor's Handbook that when patients thank us rather than each other at the end of treatment, we should ask ourselves what we have done wrong. The whole purpose of a treatment centre is educational rather than curative; recovery comes in the Anonymous Fellowships, not in treatment centres. All we can do in a treatment centre is to aim to get a larger number of people into recovery in the Anonymous Fellowships than would otherwise have been able to achieve that by going there directly rather than to treatment first. We have the opportunity to educate patients on a broad range of addictive behaviours rather than simply on the particular substance or process focused upon in a particular Anonymous Fellowship. We also have the privilege of offering an addiction-free environment for twenty-four hours a day for several weeks. Of course there will always be relapses but the whole purpose of a treatment centre is to reduce the relapse rate as far as possible. Our research team focuses upon exactly that aim of reduction of relapse rates as their prime *raison d'etre*.

We find that patients often want to have "Therapy" (with a capital "T"), something that focuses in depth upon their own special needs. This is often counter-productive. Addicts need to see what they have in common with other addicts rather than focus upon the differences. Another common quest is when patients say, "I want to find out who I am". Our reply is very straightforward: "You are who your family and friends say you are, as a result of being on the receiving end of your behaviour". Identity is not something fixed in stone; it varies from day to day, according to what we put into and take from our relationships. If we behave badly towards other people then that defines us for that time. However, we can change our behaviour and therefore change that identity. By taking on new ideas and progressively changing our behaviour towards being more considerate and understanding of other people, we should be able to say that we are not the same people that we were the previous year, let alone ten years or more ago. We grow and mature. We have no permanent identity.

Counsellors, therapists and psychotherapists (the change in terminology may reflect no more than the size of the fee charged) often make their livings by providing one-to-one sessions. It is therefore not in their financial interests for patients to get better and become independent. As mentioned, at PROMIS almost all our work is done in group therapy. The exceptions are when we give initial interviews to prospective patients and when we appoint a Focal Counsellor to remind patients on a day-to-day basis of the things that they might prefer to forget (such as their continuing nicotine addiction). Patients may want one-to-one therapy but we find that it is not very often in their best interests for them to have it. They are not special and different. They do not, any more than anyone else, have profound inner damage as a result of childhood experience. They may have been through fearful personal experiences but very often so have the other patients and it is helpful to share those experiences and recognise that recovery is possible through mutual support and encouragement rather than through dependence upon professional therapy.

Addicts love professional therapy precisely because it establishes them as being special and different. What they most commonly need is to be reminded that they are common or garden addicts and that they need to work the Twelve Step programme, the same as anyone else, rather than wallow in a sea of self-pity and blame in "Therapy", which is where compulsive helping counsellors would keep them for years.

A further risk of getting involved with compulsive helping counsellors is when early childhood experiences are examined in depth. Almost every one of us has been abused or abandoned in some way and it is only too easy to feed the addictive tendency towards blame and self-pity when focusing upon early childhood issues. Mention the word "mother" and any patient will cry – and then believe that the counsellor has profound insight and skill. Some treatment programmes set great store on examining "family of origin" issues and even in laying these out psychodramatically as a group sculpture, getting various members of the group to represent particular members of the patient's family. Again, this can awaken the addict's tendency – never far below the surface – for self-pity and blame. Our preference at PROMIS is to help patients to examine how their *own* behaviour affects other members of their family, rather than the other way round. If family of origin issues are to be examined, we recommend that patients look at their grandparents and therefore at the childhood of their own parents. In this way, they may see that their parents often did the best that they could in their particular circumstances.

For example, my mother's father died when she was six years old. Her mother was an active alcoholic and therefore my mother herself was left to provide as much care as she could for her younger sister and brother. My father's father was also alcoholic and my father, as the eldest son, left school at the age of thirteen in order to do what he could to support his mother. Being aware of that family background, I am very much aware of how much my parents gave me in comparison with what they themselves received. Ten years ago my wife, Meg, did a great deal of work on her relationship with her alcoholic father who had given her a dreadfully abusive childhood. However, he also gave her a love of music and found an excellent teacher for her so that she became an accomplished pianist by the age of thirteen. Thus, ten years ago she learnt how to focus more upon what her father had given her than upon what his disease had taken from her. He had been dead for over twenty years when she did that work on their relationship.

Thus, I believe that there is a time to examine early childhood influences but this should only be undertaken when recovery is clearly established, say, not before six years. At that time one can look back with understanding, acceptance, forgiveness and even with humour whereas at an earlier time in recovery one might again relapse into blame and self-pity. Compulsive helper counsellors will tend to want to see everything from the patient's point of view and will tend therefore to fuel the addictive disease rather than recovery, bringing out resentment and self-pity rather than acceptance and even gratitude. That is not clever.

Chapter Sixteen

The Willingness to be Helped Ourselves

Intervening in someone's compulsive helping is exceedingly difficult. Compulsive helpers do not want to receive help; they want to give it. They don't want to acknowledge their own neediness; they hate it. They want to sympathise and empathise with others; not to be on the receiving end.

When confronted in their compulsive helping behaviour, they come out fighting, saying that they are only trying to do the best they can. Indeed that is true, but none the less it can still cause a lot of damage.

The classic intervention techniques in the treatment of alcoholism and drug addiction, first formulated by the Johnson Institute in the USA, are to follow a specific protocol:

i.   I love you/I am fond of you and I am concerned for you

ii.   AND (not but – which would cancel out the love or concern)

iii.   I observe:
        a.   fact.
        b.   fact.
        c.   fact. (These must always be precise and kept as simple as possible).

iv.   I propose:
        a.   action.
        b.   action.
        c.   action. (These should also be precise and should not allow the addict to dictate his or her own terms of treatment).

v.   If you do not agree to these recommendations I shall:

        a.   action.
        b.   action.
        c.   action. (Once these threats are made, one has to be prepared to carry them out).

Sometimes interventions can be made into an extended process, taking half a day and involving family and friends, employers and doctors and heaven knows who else. The intention is to bring the addict face to face with reality. It sometimes works and it is certainly worth a try. Anything is worth a try if the progressive destruction of future years can be cut short.

The difficulty with intervening in a compulsive helper's behaviour is that the behaviour seems so absolutely reasonable and even worthy. Certainly, as previously illustrated in chapter five, there are very strong environmental and cultural influences that lead towards compulsive helping being lauded rather than criticised. We praise people who sacrifice themselves in the service of others. We rarely stop to ask whether their "help" has truly been helpful in furthering the recipient's autonomy rather than creating a dependency.

The dependency culture is a compulsive helpers' paradise, where they are needed every hour of every day for ever more, where they can fill themselves with virtue till they burst. It has become so institutionalised in the welfare state that it is sometimes believed that only cruel and uncaring people could ever challenge the ideas upon which it is based. The appreciation that people feel for services that they or their friends may have received "at no cost" in the NHS on occasions clouds their judgement. Often they do not realise that they have paid more in taxes than the service would have cost in the first place. As an insurance system, it is poor value for money. The welfare state does not rob Peter to pay Paul. There are not enough rich Peters to go around. The welfare state robs Paul, messes around at great administrative expense and then gives Paul back less than he had in the first place. It is simply not true to say that there is no alternative.

P. J. O'Rourke, in his superbly challenging book *Eat the Rich* (Picador 1999), contrasts various countries in various ways. On the subject of economy he contrasts Hong Kong, which has absolutely no natural resources whatever but has one of the highest per capita incomes in the world, and Tanzania, which has vast natural resources but is largely dependent upon foreign aid, becoming to all intents and purposes a subsidised zoo. As this illustration emphasises, contrasts in material wealth – and all that comes from that – may be more dependent upon political philosophy than anything else. The poor in the USA tend not to remain poor for very long; theirs is a highly mobile society, taking in vast numbers of immigrants at the bottom of the socio-economic scale each year and giving them opportunities for advancement. However fashionable it may be for other countries to criticise America, there is no stampede to leave that country; only to enter it.

Furthermore, the greatest advances in healthcare very often originate in the USA, the home of capitalism, rather than in socialist countries. Government Medicare and Medicaid systems in the USA do a great deal to help the elderly and the disadvantaged and the Health Care Maintenance Organisations, such as the Kaiser Permanente Scheme, attempt to provide comprehensive insurance-based care, although it has to be said that the end results sometimes mirror the worst of the British NHS. The ideas of our welfare state may appear to be worthy, to the extent of being unchallengeable, but the evidence is that they do not work in practice. Nor have they been copied to any significant degree in other countries. Compulsive helpers, when they demand the resources of the state for their own chosen causes, here and abroad, are therefore in practice working towards the destruction rather than the improvement of their societies.

The viewpoint of compulsive helpers may be very patronising. The corollary of needing to be needed is that they believe that other people do actually need them. It may not occur to them that the greatest form of help one can ever give to another person is to enable him or her to develop his or her own resources rather than receive things from other people. It seems extraordinary that means tests should be such a political *bête noire* – even though income tax is itself based upon a means test – but political compulsive helpers want to help *everybody*; they are not content simply to give state resources to those who most need them and who have the best chance of benefiting from them. This patronising, almost supercilious, attitude reveals compulsive helpers at their worst.

To be able to help compulsive helpers to desist from that specific behaviour would be greeted with incredulity. After all, they are not seen as addicts; they don't appear to do anything wrong and it is presumed that people benefit from their activities rather than suffer from them. However, they need to be challenged on each and every one of these rationalisations. They *are* addicts: their behaviour is undertaken in order to achieve mood-alteration. It *is* progressive and destructive. It does not necessarily help the recipient at all: it may be highly destructive. It also damages the compulsive helper by taking the focus – and the time and often the money as well – away from more positive and less patronising pursuits with family and friends. Just about the only positive aspect of compulsive helpers' behaviour is that their activities are legal. Perhaps the law has got it wrong, considering the damage that compulsive helpers can do!

For any addict to be prepared to receive help involves a level of humility that is rarely found. It is for precisely this reason that leaving people in the pain of their own creation may be the only stimulus that works in guiding an addict of any kind towards less destructive behaviour. This applies just as much to compulsive helpers as it does to primary addicts. Paradoxically, as it may appear, the recovering primary addicts have to help the compulsive helpers by saying "I don't need your help; it doesn't help me". After all that compulsive helpers have been through during the times when the primary addicts were using addictive substances or processes, hearing this statement from an addict in recovery can be very painful. However, this is what must be said if the relationship is to progress and if both parties are to have lives that are free from dependency of one kind or another.

Compulsive helpers can get better from their addiction by working their own Twelve Step programme in Helpers Anonymous and by learning to live their lives *alongside* other people, rather than above them or below them in psychological or social terms. As with other addicts, they need to check their ideas and behaviour with other people in recovery: in this case with other compulsive helpers. The tendency will always be for recovering compulsive helpers to want to devote their lives towards helping addicts. That is the last thing they should do; primary addicts will see them coming a mile away! If they choose to enter the professional field of counselling, they should work to help compulsive helpers. They have had the ideal training and personal experience. At last they can devote themselves to something that really is worthwhile and they really can be helpful.

Appendix

Helpers Anonymous Suggested Format for Meetings

Helpers Anonymous Suggested Format for Meetings.

(reproduced with kind permission of Helpers Anonymous).

Welcome to the meeting of Helpers Anonymous.

Shall we introduce ourselves by first names only?
My name is ... and I am a compulsive helper.
(*other members introduce themselves*).

We ask that there shall be no eating, drinking, smoking or use of any mood-altering substance during the meeting.

Shall we begin our meeting with a period of silence in which we remind ourselves of our reasons for being here? *(silence)*

Helpers Anonymous is for those who have known a feeling of despair in finding that being concerned for another person, or for many others, becomes compulsive so that it may become an obsession, never-ending and even destructive to ourselves and to others.

We have learned that this compulsion is relieved by a change in our own thoughts, feelings and behaviour, through the continued working of our Twelve Step programme of recovery, with the aid of a Higher Power, greater than ourselves, <u>as each one of us may choose to understand this.</u>

Here we learn to live comfortably in spite of unsolved problems and we learn to be genuinely helpful to others and to ourselves.

Helpers Anonymous has basic readings that are read by different members at each meeting:

1. Twelve Steps.

2. Twelve Traditions.

3. Five Fatal Flaws.

4. Helping Others.

5. The Willingness to be Helped Ourselves.

In the Big Book of Alcoholics Anonymous it states (on page 64) that "resentment is the number one offender". Therefore we do not come to meetings in order to cry over the injustices of our childhoods or compete with each other in telling fearful stories of our past lives and present miseries, blaming others and pitying ourselves. Rather, we take our own inventory and we share our experience (both good and bad), strength and hope in such away as to encourage newcomers and set a positive example of recovery. Anything you hear in the meeting is strictly the opinion of each individual speaker. If any member says something with which you disagree or with which you feel upset, please remember that he or she is speaking only from his or her own experience and not on behalf of Helpers Anonymous. We have a list of telephone numbers of members who are happy to be contacted between meetings. Please take such numbers as you may wish and add your own number, if you wish to do so.

Announcements.
Do we have any announcements?
<u>Introduction</u> to the Step study, topic for discussion, or guest speaker.

Closing
The principles of Helpers Anonymous are found in our Twelve Steps and Twelve Traditions. Our <u>seventh tradition</u> states that each group should be fully self-supporting. While no dues or fees are required for membership, and especially not from newcomers, our voluntary contributions are used to pay for rent and literature, as well as allowing us to carry the message of our programme to others through the continued support of the Helpers Anonymous Service Office.

(wait until all contributions are collected)

Our <u>ninth step</u> states "Made direct amends to those we had harmed except when to do so would injure them or others." The Big Book of Alcoholics Anonymous (on page 83) <u>in dealing with this ninth step</u> makes the following promises: "If we are painstaking about this phase of our development, we will be amazed before we are half way through. We are going to know a new freedom and a new happiness. We will not regret the past nor wish to shut the door on it. We will comprehend the word serenity and we will know peace. No matter how far down the scale we have gone, we will see how our experience can benefit others. That feeling of uselessness and self-pity will disappear. We will lose interest in selfish things and gain interest in our fellows. Self-seeking will slip away. Our whole attitude and outlook upon life will change. Fear of people and of economic insecurity will leave us. We will intuitively know how to handle situations which used to baffle us. We will suddenly realise that God is doing for us what we could not do for ourselves."

Shall we close our meeting with the Serenity Prayer?

God grant me the serenity
To accept the things I cannot change,
Courage to change the things I can
And the wisdom to know the difference.

(Excerpt from page 64 and The Promises from Page 83 of " Alcoholics Anonymous" reprinted with permission of Alcoholics Anonymous World Services Inc.)

Helpers Anonymous Twelve Steps.

Here are the steps we took, which are suggested as a programme of recovery:

1. We admitted we were powerless over other people's lives and our own compulsive helping and that our lives had become unmanageable.

2. Came to believe that a power greater than ourselves could restore us to sanity.

3. Made a decision to turn our will and our lives over to the care of God _as we understood Him_.

4. Made a searching and fearless moral inventory of ourselves.

5. Admitted to God, to ourselves and to another human being the exact nature of our wrongs.

6. Were entirely ready to have God remove all these defects of character.

7. Humbly asked Him to remove our shortcomings.

8. Made a list of all persons we had harmed, and became willing to make amends to them all.

9. Made direct amends to such people wherever possible, except when to do so would injure them or others.

10. Continued to take personal inventory and when we were wrong promptly admitted it.

11. Sought through prayer and meditation to improve our conscious contact with God, _as we understood Him_, praying only for knowledge of His will for us and the power to carry that out.

12. Having had a spiritual awakening as a result of these steps we tried to carry this message to compulsive helpers who still suffer, and to practise these principles in all our affairs.

Helpers Anonymous Twelve Traditions

1. Our common welfare should come first; personal progress for the greatest number depends upon unity.

2. For our group purposes there is but one authority – a loving God, as He may express Himself in our group conscience. Our leaders are but trusted servants – they do not govern.

3. Individuals concerned with helping others in any way and concerned with their own compulsive helping, when gathered together for mutual aid, may call themselves a Helpers Anonymous group provided that, as a group, they have no other affiliation. The only requirement for membership is a desire to cease compulsive helping.

4. Each group should be autonomous, except in matters affecting other groups or Helpers Anonymous as a whole.

5. Each group has but one primary purpose, to carry its message to the compulsive helper who still suffers.

6. Helpers Anonymous groups should never endorse, finance, or lend our name to any outside enterprise, lest problems of money, property and prestige divert us from our primary purpose.

7. Every group should be fully self-supporting, declining outside contributions.

8. Helpers Anonymous Twelfth Step work should remain forever non-professional, but our service centres may employ special workers.

9. Our groups, as such, should never be organised, but we may create service boards or committees directly responsible to the groups they serve.

10. Helpers Anonymous has no opinion on outside issues; hence our name should never be drawn into public controversy.

11. Our public relations policies are based on attraction rather than promotion; we should always maintain personal anonymity at the level of press, radio, films and TV. We need to guard with special care the anonymity of our members, as well as those of other recovery programmes.

12. Anonymity is the spiritual foundation of all our Traditions, ever reminding us to place principles before personalities.

HELPERS ANONYMOUS: FIVE FATAL FLAWS

Addictive disease is cunning, baffling and powerful: Anonymous Fellowships are fragile. If our meetings and our Fellowship of Helpers Anonymous are to survive and flourish, they need the life of recovery breathed into them and we should beware of five fatal flaws:

The first is arrogance. We make no rules on how any individual member should work his or her programme of recovery. Even the Twelve Steps are merely suggested. We avoid any discussion of religion, politics or therapeutic programmes, remembering that these are "outside issues" as far as Helpers Anonymous is concerned.

The second is betrayal. We share our thoughts, feelings and experiences in confidence and in anonymity.

The third is dominance. All members of Helpers Anonymous, including newcomers, have equal status. Any form of service to the groups or to the Fellowship itself is a privilege and a position of trust rather than authority.

The fourth is the use of "therapeutic jargon". For example, we avoid the use of words or phrases such as "Co-Dependency", "Inner child" or "Anger work" that may mean different things to different people and hence cause confusion and divert us from our goal of spiritual recovery. Many members of various Twelve Step Programmes have individually benefited from specific ideas or therapies of one kind or another. Other members have not benefited and may even have been discouraged. Therefore, in order to maintain the cohesion of our groups, we refer during meetings only to the ideas and principles of the Twelve Steps.

The fifth is insensitivity. We avoid eating, drinking, smoking or using any other mood-altering substance or process during meetings. This use may be insensitive to other members. It may also blunt our own feelings and therefore damage our full capacity to benefit from any message of recovery. In Helpers Anonymous we believe that dependence upon mood-altering substances or processes is best acknowledged and helped through Addictions Anonymous, or other appropriate Anonymous Fellowships, rather than accommodated.

Helping Others

In Helpers Anonymous we learn through the Twelve Steps how to be genuinely helpful to others and avoid being compulsive helpers. We learn how to care and not care-take.

To help other people is a lovely thing. To be kind and considerate, supportive and generous, is beautiful.

These are the building bricks of a good life. In giving to others, we ourselves receive the gifts of happiness and contentment.

Yet this very process, the basis of honest and loving relationships, is corrupted by addictive disease. The more we give the more the addict takes and demands, and then we feel we should give even more. Each of us, the addict and the helper, is hooked into the other's compulsive behaviour in a dreadful dance.

In Helpers Anonymous we learn to see the difference between helping the person and aiding and abetting his or her addictive disease by our own inappropriate action or inaction. We learn to take the risk of leaving the addict to take full responsibility for the consequences of his or her own decisions and behaviour. Throughout all the good times and bad we respect the rights of the individual addict to make his or her own choices, regardless of how ill advised or damaging we may perceive those choices to be. We recognise that addictive disease is not the fault of the sufferer and we continue to respect or love the individual regardless of the decisions and actions taken. While we reject addictive behaviour and we hold the addict to full account for all his or her actions, we still do not reject the human being from our minds or hearts.

We learn to encourage his or her steps towards recovery, not through believing promises or offering bribes for changes in future behaviour, but through responding to consistent and progressive change that is actually achieved. We learn to be deaf to the self-pity and blaming of addictive disease, while responding positively to genuine attempts at change in thoughts, feelings and behaviour through working a Twelve Step programme of recovery. Yet at all times we continue our respect or love, even in the face of the very opposite of our own advice, belief or hope.

In Helpers Anonymous we also come to see that to be of real help to others we must first be willing to be helped ourselves by coming to understand our <u>own</u> addictive nature as compulsive helpers and treat this, one day at a time, through our <u>own</u> Twelve Step programme of recovery.

compulsive helping

The Willingness to be Helped Ourselves

When we first come to Helpers Anonymous our concern is mostly for someone else, We search for new ideas on how to help the ones we love or for whom we are concerned. We want to understand new theories of addiction or of compulsive and destructive behaviour. We seek out new experts to advise us. In our desperation we will listen to anybody, go anywhere, and do almost anything.

Grabbing enthusiastically at each new "solution", we become thrilled with the hope that at last we have found someone who "really knows" and something that "really works". But each time, when the honeymoon period wears off, we become sad and disillusioned – until the next time; until we find the next idea and the next expert. Then off we go yet again in our determined and exhausting search,

But then even this new idea turns out to be no good and even this new expert is no wiser than the last. Certainly there are times – perhaps lasting weeks, months or even more – when things seem to be working out really well. We try to be calm, confident, hopeful and encouraging but inside there may still be the same old fears: "Is he going to go back to it one day?", "Is she in trouble again?", "Why did he do that?", "What is that so-called friend of hers doing now?", "Suppose it all goes wrong again?".

We learn from painful experience not to ask these questions out loud. But we say to ourselves that surely it is too much to ask that we shouldn't <u>think</u> these things. Anyway, surely, it's our <u>responsibility</u> as a family member or friend, employer or counsellor, to be concerned about these things. Isn't it?

Then, at last, when we hear the stories told in Helpers Anonymous, we know one thing for certain: these people have been where we have been; they know our fears and hopes from the inside.

But the more we listen, the more we are struck by one particular feature: in Helpers Anonymous the members talk little about the addicts in their lives and they talk much about their own behaviour. They openly acknowledge that they work the Twelve Step programme of recovery from addiction <u>for themselves</u> and not simply because they want to understand it for someone else.

Reflecting on our <u>own</u> behaviour, many of us recognise two things:
i.   We have been care-taking for other people, wanting them to need us, for as long as we can remember, certainly for longer than we have been trying to help the particular person who brought us to Helpers Anonymous.

ii. We may have neglected other people, and other responsibilities, and we have damaged ourselves and the quality of our own lives.

These two characteristics – care-taking and self-denial – have been dominant features of our lives and, in truth, they have not helped in the way we wished and they have certainly led to a lot of damage in our own lives.

At first, we may be angry at having the spotlight turned on our own behaviour – just as any addict reacts in exactly this way. In time we come to ask ourselves "Did my hive of activity <u>really</u> help? Conversely, was it <u>really</u> true, as I thought, that I did not try hard enough? However hard I tried, wasn't there <u>always</u> one more idea and one more expert?".

We come to see that we have ourselves been caught up in our own addictive behaviour. Care-taking and self-denial have become progressive and destructive in just the same way and to the same extent as any other addictive process is progressive and destructive.

Here in Helpers Anonymous, just as in any other Anonymous Fellowship for any other form of addictive disease, we learn to look at our <u>own</u> behaviour and we gradually learn to be helped ourselves.

Alcoholics Anonymous Twelve Steps

1. We admitted we were powerless over alcohol – that our lives had become unmanageable.

2. Came to believe that a Power greater than ourselves could restore us to sanity.

3. Made a decision to turn our will and our lives over to the care of God as we understood Him.

4. Made a searching and fearless moral inventory of ourselves.

5. Admitted to God, to ourselves and to another human being the exact nature of our wrongs.

6. Were entirely ready to have God remove all these defects of character.

7. Humbly asked Him to remove our shortcomings.

8. Made a list of all persons we had harmed, and became willing to make amends to them all.

9. Made direct amends to such people wherever possible, except when to do so would injure them or others.

10. Continued to take personal inventory and when we were wrong promptly admitted it.

11. Sought through prayer and meditation to improve our conscious contact with God, <u>*as we understood Him*</u>, praying only for knowledge of His will for us and the power to carry that out.

12. Having had a spiritual awakening as the result of these steps, we tried to carry this message to alcoholics who still suffer and to practise these principles in all our affairs.

The Twelve Steps are reprinted with the permission of Alcoholics Anonymous World Service, Inc. Permission to reprint and adapt the Twelve Steps does not mean that AA is in any way affiliated with this programme. AA is a programme of recovery from alcoholism – use of the Twelve Steps in connection with programmes and activities, which are patterned after AA, but which address other problems, does not imply otherwise.

compulsive helping

Alcoholics Anonymous Twelve Traditions

1. Our common welfare should come first; personal recovery depends upon AA unity.

2. For our group purpose, there is but one ultimate authority – a loving God as He may express Himself in our group conscience Our leaders are but trusted servants; they do not govern.

3. The only requirement for AA membership is a desire to stop drinking.

4. Each group should be autonomous except in matters affecting other groups or AA as a whole.

5. Each group has but one primary purpose – to carry its message to the alcoholic who still suffers.

6. An AA group ought never endorse, finance, or lend the AA name to any related facility or outside enterprise, lest problems of money, property and prestige divert us from our primary purpose.

7. Every AA group ought to be fully self-supporting; declining outside contributions.

8. Alcoholics Anonymous should remain forever non-professional but our service centres may employ special workers.

9. AA, as such, ought never be organised; but we may create service boards or committees directly responsible to those they serve.

10. Alcoholics Anonymous has no opinion on outside issues; hence the AA name ought never to be drawn into public controversy.

11. Our public relations policy is based on attraction rather than promotion; we need always maintain personal anonymity at the level of press, radio, films and TV.

12. Anonymity is the spiritual foundation of all our traditions, ever reminding us to place principles before personalities.

The Twelve Traditions are reprinted with the permission of Alcoholics Anonymous World Service, Inc. Permission to reprint and adapt the Twelve Steps does not mean that AA is in any way affiliated with this programme. AA is a programme of recovery from alcoholism – use of the Twelve Steps in connection with programmes and activities, which are patterned after AA, but which address other problems, does not imply otherwise.

Other books in the series

Preventing Addiction

Cigarette Smoking. Fifteen reasons for continuing to smoke (or not)

Healing

Common Sense in the Treatment of Eating Disorders

Spiritual Awakening. Working the Twelve Step programme

Inside the Madness

How to Combat Alcoholism and Addiction

How to Combat Anorexia, Bulimia and Compulsive Overeating

Spirituality for Atheists and Agnostics

A New Life. Healing depression

Compulsive Helping

Healthy Relationships

Prescription Drug Addiction. My doctor gave it to me

Behavioural Addictions: Workaholism. Shopaholism. Exercise Addiction. Gambling and Risk Taking. Self-Harming. Obsessive Compulsive Disorder

False Medical Gods

Detoxification and Harm Minimisation

Childhood Abuse and Abandonment

Healing Emotional Trauma with E.M.D.R.

Healing Emotional Trauma with Psychodrama

Treating Chronic Relapse. Not again

Help: The Dairy of a Private Doctor

> **Vol 1: I will *not* make do.** The philosophy and politics of help

> **Vol 2: Daughters are Difficult.** Professional help in clinical practice

> **Vol 3: Henry is a Good Man.** The boundaries of help

> **Vol 4: Robin's turn.** Beyond help